Wandering in Costa Rica
Landscapes Lost and Found

WANDERING IN COSTA RICA
Landscapes Lost and Found

Edited by
Joanna Biggar &
Linda Watanabe McFerrin

Wanderland Writers
Oakland, California

Copyright © 2010 Wanderland Writers. All rights reserved.

For permission to print essays in this volume, grateful acknowledgement is made to the holders of copyright named on pages 170 – 179.

Photographs
Front cover:
Red-lored parrot ©Laurie McAndish King
Back cover:
Macaw, flower, monkey ©Laurie McAndish King
Landscape ©JM Shubin
Interior photos:
Page 64 ©Linda Watanabe McFerrin; page 72 ©Robin Kazmier; page 124 ©Walter Gavitt Ferguson; page 179 ©Alison Wright; all others ©JMShubin & Laurie McAndish King.

Cover design, interior design, map, and photosketches by JM Shubin, www.bookalchemist.net
Typefaces: Sabon, Garamond, Shinn

CATALOGING DATA:
Wandering in Costa Rica: Landscapes Lost and Found
Edited by Linda Watanabe McFerrin and Joanna Biggar

ISBN: 978-0-9981960-8-4

To *Amigos de las Aves* and all others who are working to preserve the wildlife and natural wonders of Costa Rica.

Contents

Map	9
Introduction	10
In the Nest Lenny Karpman	13
Sueño Azul Sandra Bracken	19
A Coffin Rises Linda Coffin	23
Let's Not Go There Nancy Alpert	31
Stravinsky's Gift Laurie McAndish King	39
Terror in Escazú Carol McCool	49
Peaceable Kingdom M.J. Pramik	55
Costa Rica Animals Thanasis Maskaleris	63
Ten Tiny Tico Tips for Travelers Joanna Biggar	65
River Crossing Robin Kazmier	73

Quetzal Quest Linda Watanabe McFerrin	85
Lost Quetzal in San Francisco Thanasis Maskaleris	89
Facing Luís Carol McCool	91
Dodging Snakes in Costa Rica Anne Sigmon	101
Pepé LeCoon Greg Bascom	113
The King of Calypso Joanna Biggar	125
Cocooning in Costa Rica Linda Watanabe McFerrin	137
Downtime Sandra Bracken	143
Roots and Branches Carol McCool	151
Chickens and Zippers Lenny Karpman	157
Lenny, After the Storm Joanna Biggar	163
Glossary	166
Author biographies	168
Editor biographies	176

Costa Rica

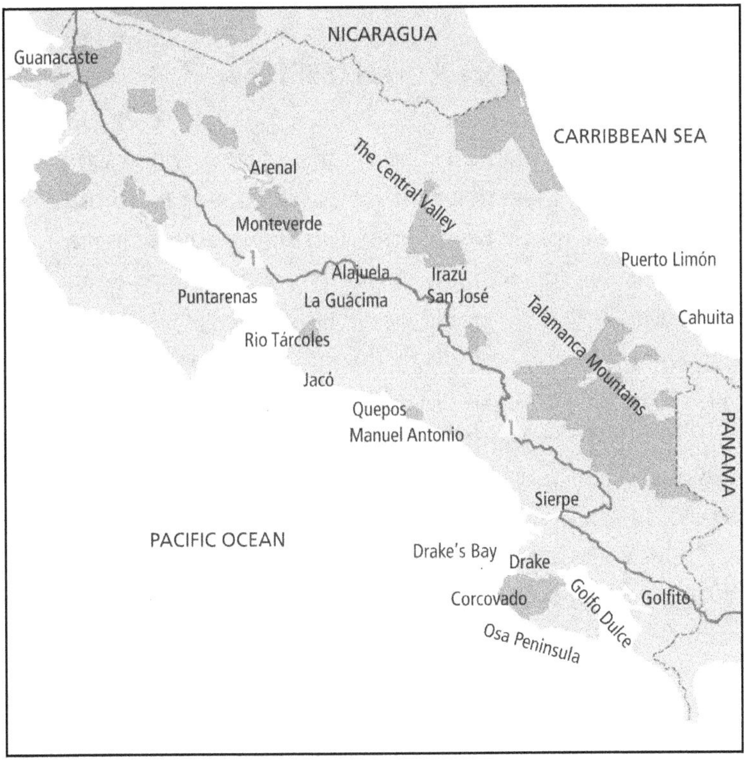
NICARAGUA
Guanacaste
CARRIBBEAN SEA
Arenal
The Central Valley
Monteverde
Puerto Limón
Alajuela
Irazú
Puntarenas
La Guácima
San José
Talamanca Mountains
Cahuita
Rio Tárcoles
Jacó
Quepos
Manuel Antonio
PANAMA
Sierpe
PACIFIC OCEAN
Drake's Bay
Drake
Corcovado
Golfo Dulce
Golfito
Osa Peninsula

Introduction

It began with a magical place, in this case a friend's *finca* in La Guácima, a small town in Costa Rica. How could we resist when expat writer, Lenny Karpman, and his wife, Joan Hall, invited us to lead a workshop in their "peaceable kingdom"?

As we gathered a baker's dozen of our favorite travelers and writers we had no idea how transformative the journey would be. We were nurtured and inspired in an environment beyond compare. Our host, *Don* Lenny, says it best in his story "In the Nest."

"Thou shalt not" is no longer posted atop the gate. Flowers of all colors and fragrances emerge anew with each sunrise. When blossoms fall, it is only to make way for the coming of fruit.

Our stories are that fruit. Wandering from that nest, as a group and individually, we gathered tales from across the country. From rainforests, volcanoes, tropical beaches, butterfly gardens, colorful towns and villages and other areas in this land we have come to know as a kind of Eden, our little troupe of writers brought together a cornucopia of very personal records of their experiences. The characters who populate these pages are among the greatest gifts that Costa Rica offered us.

As writers and teachers we were privileged to be in such a place and in such company.

—Linda Watanabe McFerrin and Joanna Biggar,
Oakland, California

In the Nest

Lenny Karpman

"Let be be finale of seem.
The only emperor is the emperor of ice-cream."
—*Wallace Stevens*

On my farm in Costa Rica, I see morning clouds racing in the wind across the face of the mountain dressed in amber and pink. Wind chimes serenade. A white rooster bellows majestically. The chorus of parrots screeches for attention. I savor a cup of rich coffee that jump-starts my taste buds, widens my eyes and slides warmth down my throat. The sweet smell of ylang ylang blossoms fills my nostrils. The nest is alive.

I am Lenny to my Gringo friends, *miel* (honey) to my wife, *Don Leni* to Costa Rican *amigos*, dad to the kids and grandpa to the parrots and my human grandkids. Those

Wandering in Costa Rica: Landscapes Lost and Found

names define me through the filter of their eyes and thoughts but offer little clarity to the nameless one I seek inside me. Occasionally brief glimpses of him emerge.

I remember the sensation of the warmth from summer sun penetrating the depth of my body as I lay supine on the flat concrete slab that bordered the front steps to our home when I was four. I felt enriched, secure and very happy. Perhaps ten years later I felt a similar sensation. My dog and I had run miles through Keeney Park in Hartford. We sprawled on a patch of earthy newly mowed grass. He rested his chin on my chest and snored gently. I dozed as well, until a green caterpillar tickled among the blond hairs of my arm. My nameless self awoke feeling free and powerful. My dog wagged his tail in helicopter rotation and ran alongside me out of the park toward home. I bobbed and weaved around trees and telephone poles with an imaginary football tucked under one arm, spun past a fire hydrant off tackle into the open field, and bounded up the front porch stairs three at a time. Nameless died there.

"You're late for dinner. Lenny! Go wash your hands."

I gestured King to follow me inside. His tail hung motionless. My nameless boy remained interred for decades.

I marched mechanically through adolescence and into adulthood, nearly always doing as I was told. After medical school, I became Dr. Karpman to my patients and to myself.

In my early forties I, Lenny/Dr. Karpman, sat on a grassy knoll and watched another nameless young boy stutter-step down the sidewalk, whistling loudly, dragging sneaker laces through puddles, kicking a soccer ball disguised as a stone down a surrogate field, index finger in his nose. A woman passed him by. He saw her see him. Finger fled nose. His whistling stopped abruptly. Both arms dropped to his sides. Nameless remembered who he was supposed to be. Head down, with rigid gait, he walked like a robot past the abandoned stone and self. I saw who I had once been and wept.

In my mid-fifties, I suffered an unknown illness. I had memory problems that scared the hell out of me. My medical caregivers called it dementia. Luckily, they were wrong. The malady faded over time but left a legacy. In its wake, I had to come to terms with my demons: death and dying. Once past their gray pall, I felt lighter, freer. Whatever demons emerge in the future, I will know them when I see them and will face them without fear.

Now, in the November of my life, I reside in Costa Rica's Central Valley. "Thou shalt not" is no longer posted atop the gate. Flowers of all colors and fragrances emerge anew with each sunrise. When blossoms fall, it is only to make way for the coming of fruit. Chicks hatch. Dogs lick and cats rub with unqualified affection. Life renews unfettered.

I share my nest with every fluffy hatchling I see in every tree, applaud their courage and determination as they rock on the edge of their straw nursery and dare to fly for the first time. Jubilation. In time, I might fly.

A wood stork grabs my gaze and softens shrill resolve into murmuring chant. It floats free on air currents above the mango trees and palms, white with black-tipped wings that move without effort. Its leading graceful neck and trailing long legs balance. I watch as it turns upward and outward into vastness and freedom.

Sueño Azul

Sandra Bracken

ez vela stirs in the sapphire blue before dawn—
the sailfish.
Our unforgettable dance years ago
became the prelude to my return,
so spirited our encounter
so strong the allure of place.

Where I endure the throat-closing fumes
that cloud city air until
the roar of jet engines grows distant
and barely remembered
amid the soft sighs of doves and nesting parakeets.
Chatter between parrots rises to deafening
takes flight on the wind.

The wind propels bamboo chimes
into fitful hammering
drums with branches a wild riff on the roof.
Fierce and strong it pushes me
walking off the road.
Yet every plant has its wind song.

Wandering in Costa Rica: Landscapes Lost and Found

In this world of textural pleasures
my fingers caress tender buds and velvet blossoms
growing from tough stems with crusty pods.
Familiar ferns brush my legs
my *abuela's* fern.
Lacy beams of light
burn through overlapping patterns of green,
are reflected over and over.

Flashes of *azul* are elusive but real—
indigo macaw ... blue morpho butterfly
there ... not there
wait.

I waited for *pez vela*.
He surged
held his position above the water
swaying seductively.
His midnight-blue brilliance changed each time,
took on a copper over-glow.
His piercing stare hypnotizing.

Colors change in the late afternoon garden—
purple to black, orange to earth tones.
The wind has softened.
Under flowered arbors a path leads
to a bench where I sit as evening unfolds.
Subdued sounds spill into the quiet—
rustling palms and
a small flock of parrots settling to roost.

Just beyond the edge of shadows
a fragile ribbon of blue shimmers in and out of sight.
Wings folded, mottled brown
tracings in black and white
hidden on the surface of a palm,
the butterfly plays hide and seek.
I wait.

Opening his wings
he rises in a whisper of iridescent flight.
Transfixed, I follow the blue morpho butterfly
into the violet dusk
thinking
pez vela.

A Coffin Rises

Linda Coffin

Drool! Slurp! Slobber!
   I awake to the vision of six long, wet tongues. Drool and slobber rained down on me like a day in the rainforest. What an introduction to Costa Rica and *Finca Fango de la Suerte*!
   Surrounding my prone body are six very friendly dogs of every description—large, small, black, white, brown, multi-colored. They dance around me excitedly. After all, I am their afternoon's entertainment.
   "Stop."
   "Get back."
   "No licking."
   "Ms. Coffin, are you okay?"
   Somehow I had gone from riding in an ancient Hyundai van that rattled, rocked and rolled from one side of the road to the other, to lying face up in a bed of ferns and yellow orchids. The vision of emergency rooms, casting of broken bones, and spending the next seven days flat on my back

Wandering in Costa Rica: Landscapes Lost and Found

flashed before my eyes. My Costa Rica vacation lay in ruins.

To make matters worse, as I lie buried by vegetation, I also remember what a well-traveled friend told me about one of Costa Rica's famous and deadly snakes: the *terciopelo* or fer-de-lance, which could be found on the grounds of this same hacienda. Now visions of an appalling death by venom bite fill my mind.

My adventure had begun an hour earlier when I was met at the Juan Santamaría Airport in San José by my host, an expatriate doctor from San Francisco, in a decrepit van that looked left over from the 1960's Summer of Love.

I had taken an exhausting overnight flight from San Francisco to arrive at a decent pick-up time for my host. I suffer from a variety of physical ailments: I walk with a cane, have two knee replacements, and am recuperating from an auto accident that tore my rotator cup. Since I now have difficulty waking long distances, I request a wheelchair at the arrival gate when I fly.

This state of physical decay was not always the case.

I once galloped through airports. I had been voted "best athlete" in my high school days. Years followed with me playing tennis, golf, softball, volleyball, soccer, rock climbing, sailing, skiing, scuba diving, and then trying to learn how to surf and sailboard.

But now I stagger off the plane to find no wheelchair is available.

The girl at the arrival gates tells me, "All the lame tourists have taken them and not brought them back" (my translation). I imagine every second person in Costa Rica sits in a wheelchair and carries a cane.

However, after I conduct a lengthy hand show with another airport hostess, each of us speaking each other's native language badly, Jacinto, a very hefty *Tico*, appears to ease my rather hefty body into a procured wheelchair. Minutes later Jacinto wheels me through customs, and I am soon sitting outside in the bright blue Costa Rican sunshine, awaiting my host.

I remember his last humorous e-mail to me with directions on the pick up: "Look for an old gray bear wearing a pink polo shirt." Well, at least I should easily recognize him.

But outside, I discover not one, not two, but at least ten pink shirts. It looks like an Avon breast cancer marathon is in town. I hope the doctor isn't one of the pink-shirted males I am viewing. They all look like they lost that marathon—a little blurry-eyed, with sun-burnt faces and an "under the weather" appearance. I begin to consider jumping back on the plane and returning home.

Finally two English-speaking women approach me and tell me to sit still, that the doctor is circling in his van looking for parking. A once-white van pulls up, and a pink-shirted man with twinkly blue eyes and curly gray hair and beard leaps out and shakes my hand, saying, "Ms. Coffin, I am Lenny, your host."

The voice I hear is warm and full of natural humor.

Wandering in Costa Rica: Landscapes Lost and Found

Mentally, I cancel my flight home for my planned week at this man's hacienda and Costa Rica.

The luggage stowed, I hop with my walking stick into the van's back seat and watch Lenny work his way through San José traffic to a small town called La Guácima.

And what roads! Costa Rica proudly advertises its great infrastructure, especially the road system, in all the tourist brochures I read before coming, but its pot-holed and lumpy back roads are bone-rattling, especially in a van devoid of shocks.

Lenny leans back over the seat to give me a quick Costa Rican driver's education, "Ticos are extremely courteous, but they see no reason for using your rules of the road," as I gasped when two scooters whipped around us on different sides of the van. "The towns are full of one-way bridges, and not everyone knows the rule of alternating traffic on the bridge, so you can wait a long time before getting your chance to cross over."

I nod, whimpering under my breath. "The back roads appear to be wide enough for only one car?"

"Everyone gets along pretty well, diving in and out of ditches to avoid the bigger cars and trucks. But the most fun is when a car just stops in the middle of a street without using any signals so that the driver can converse with a friend or run in and shop for something," Lenny yells back at me.

By the time we approach our destination I am quite happy with this "devil-may-care" style of driving.

After about thirty minutes of hip, hop, bang and stop, we arrive at *Finca Fango de la Suerte*. I remember exiting the van, already admiring dozens of tropical fruit trees and a huge butterfly palm. I step down onto what I think is a tiled driveway.

My next conscious memory is that of the slurping sextet staring down at me.

I apparently missed the tiled driveway and fell into a narrow flowerbed filled with decorative rocks. The doctor and two guests from the hacienda claimed I made a grand karate fall—twisting my head to miss the tile and sliding effortlessly into the ferns and other tropical plants. Unfortunately, a major portion of my rump hit the biggest and most decorative rock.

The fall may have looked graceful to outside participants, but I saw stars and momentarily blacked out. As things came back into focus, all I could think of was spending my week in Costa Rica either in the hospital or recovering from a concussion.

As noted earlier, I am not in the best shape—actually retirement has caused me to lose any shape I ever had. I should have come to Costa Rica for a complete body makeover, not a vacation.

My host and two guests rush around to help me out of the flowerbed, but my feet are up in the air, and my head is nestling on a brilliant yellow orchid. The trio, however, know nothing of my bruised and battered body. Lenny grabs the torn shoulder while the other two try to haul me up from the ground by sheer brute strength, not knowing of my injuries or that fact that I probably outweigh all three of them. I move upward six inches and I'm let back down quickly by my three rescuers. They are kind enough not to mention my weight, but one look at their shocked faces tells me that after this trip I need to visit Weight Watchers or Jenny Craig and lose some poundage.

The brute strength maneuver is a failure. Next, they try rolling me over to my side and onto the sidewalk. This log-rolling maneuver finally works after three tries. But again, I still need to get up or spend the next seven days on the sidewalk. Finally, several cushions are brought out and placed near my knees.

I try rising up using the cushions to protect my sore knees. I call this the "car-jack-up" maneuver. I throw my good hand and arm down to the ground and from this three-point maneuver, my abs talk to my thighs, and I rise. It has taken thirty minutes, but I am upright.

Leading my rescuers and my pack of excited new canine friends, I limp to the hacienda's front door. In my previous flying days, I remember the old coda of pilots: Any landing you walk away from is successful.

Let's Not Go There

Nancy Alpert

*I*f I couldn't relax and enjoy life in the tropical paradise of Costa Rica, I wondered if, perhaps, it was time to increase my antidepressants. After all, which one of my friends wouldn't kill for the opportunity to visit this Central American oasis instead of drudging along at work for the week? But I'm pretty much the anxious type. And I'm *not* the outdoorsy-sporty type—unless you count walking from the car into Costco to buy a Liz Claiborne outfit for the plane ride an active sport, which I do. Earlier in the year, I'd passed on a singles' trip to Costa Rica because of the intimidating itinerary of zip-lining, white-water rafting, jungle-trekking and other thrills. To my credit, I'd made strides in recent years, even purchasing a tent (from Costco) and using it three times (once in my living room.) But adventure travel? No thanks. A writing workshop spent sitting indoors for hours, with ancillary trips to a butterfly farm and a bird-watching walk led by an eighty year old? No problem. I signed up.

Wandering in Costa Rica: Landscapes Lost and Found

During my first twenty-four hours in La Guácima, just northwest of San José, I found many deterrents to tranquility. The ferocious *Vientos de Navidad*, or winds, had stayed long past Christmas, and seemed capable of shoving a tree through our residence's roof. (It did tear off over thirty roofs in a nearby village.) The cacophony of four verbose parrots on the patio interfered with any attempt at relaxed outdoor dining, but at least *they* only chattered during the day. In contrast, number one on the list of "Obstacles to Nancy's Quest for Enjoyment" was the penetrating and repetitive rant of the rooster at an ungodly pre-dawn hour. Our hosts were so gracious. I began to wonder if they'd mind if I killed their cock.

That first morning, after sitting through a satisfying two-hour workshop, I traveled with the group to the Butterfly Farm, not more than ten minutes from our beautiful *finca*. Surrounded by foliage and flutter, the young guide, Dani, short for Daniela, enhanced our knowledge of the butterfly's lifecycle, anatomy and symbolism. We scouted out examples of tiny eggs, fuzzy and often homely caterpillars, dangling pupae and variegated butterflies. The malachite, halloween, monarch, tiger and the iconic blue morpho butterflies mesmerized me with their fragile flitting.

"The female butterfly mates one time in her life, but that mating can last for four hours." Dani stated this shocking fact about butterfly sex in a matter-of-fact tone. We turned to watch two butterflies entwined in the act on a piece of wire mesh. With howling winds that made it hard to hear, Dani continued, "The male mates as frequently as he can." Of course, Tiger Woods came to mind immediately, but then I got to thinking about the female's marathon sex act and the ratio of her life (three weeks, or 504 hours) to her time participating in sex, and just where I would fit into that equation, and exactly how long it had been since I'd even found a suitable mate, and where in heaven's sake exactly might I ever again meet someone I'd even want to think about mating with, and ... but let's not go there.

I was in Costa Rica to relax and enjoy myself, after all, so I refocused on the beautiful colors of these transformed creatures, and before I knew it, the butterfly female we'd just examined up close had alighted on my arm. Dani said, "It's a lucky sign to have a butterfly land on you." I did feel chosen, but then, I also felt pretty damn uncomfortable as Madame Butterfly's little fingernails (OK, so we didn't learn that much anatomy) squeezed my arm. I guess she needed that strong grasp when mating in gale force winds for four hours with her one true soul mate ... oh, never mind. I slept poorly that night, and woke up to the rooster's crow.

Again the next day, incessant winds wreaked havoc on my hair and ruffled my attempted calm. More significantly, the fierce gusts threatened real danger as I walked a two-foot sidewalk across the Rio Tárcoles Bridge to view the mud-caked crocodiles below. I pictured the gusts sweeping me into oncoming traffic or over the railings to the murky croc-

Wandering in Costa Rica: Landscapes Lost and Found

infested waters below. I shot my few photos and hurried back to the dilapidated van. Peril averted, we continued on the road another hour to Playa Blanca on the Pacific Ocean.

No sooner had my blood pressure lowered and I was beginning to unwind, than the shock absorber-less van hit one of the ubiquitous speed bumps at regular speed, and our unlucky backseat riders catapulted into the ceiling. One of our intrepid leaders, Linda, heard her vertebrae crack. We heard her answer our concern with an uncharacteristically faint voice, "No, I'm not OK."

I sat next to her on the ride back, held her hand briefly, then tried to respect her space. She stared straight ahead, looking pale and smaller than her usual shrimpy 5'2" self. I knew she was worried about a possible head injury, which plunged me into recalling exactly one year before when I witnessed my mom with her eyes rolled back emit a sickening gurgled snore as she lay unconscious following a fall. She ended up in the ICU for a week and I watched her suffer excruciating pain from bleeding on the brain, and held her hand, wondering if she would ever again be my same mama, and if I would prefer that she die rather than suffer, and I stayed in the house with my dad and cried at every piece of paper I saw with her writing on it, and worried about the shape she might come home in, and realized that one day she wouldn't come home ... but *please*, let's not go there.

I was in Costa Rica to relax and enjoy myself, after all,

so I refocused on the camaraderie of friends, my daring swimsuit change on the beach shielded only by a sarong held by Sandra, the delicious memory of my *coco* (coconut) and *vaniglia* gelato in the surfer town of Jacó, and the bright yellow/orange sunset that we writers were playfully characterizing as papaya, peach, saffron and mango orange—sport for writers. In a town called Atenas, which looked nothing like Athens, Greece, we ate *pupusas*, and life started looking better again.

The next morning, having slept decently in spite of the rooster's attempts, I ate breakfast with Sandra, my beach wardrober/accomplice. She made the comment, "You can't stop responding to the world around you—it's a matter of how you do it." Her words gave me solace and validated my inner squawking while reminding me that I had some power over it. I didn't want to live my life like a chicken. I wanted to live up to a quote I'd always loved: Helen Keller's, "Life is either a daring adventure or nothing."

With those thoughts in mind, I committed to an act not generally present in my repertoire—voluntarily rising early. I determined to get up at the crack of dawn, beat the darn cock at his game and go wake *him* up. I was going to get up at 5:30 am. To be honest, it was for the birds. Birdwatching with an eighty-year-old guide, to be exact.

I woke before my iPhone chirped its alarm and counted the seconds between cock-a-doodle-doos. Six seconds. It was not entirely dark out, and the wind had died. I put on the same

Wandering in Costa Rica: Landscapes Lost and Found

clothes as the day before, figuring I didn't have to care how I looked at that hour. Strangely, the rooster no longer crowed, as if I were his only responsibility and now he could now retire. Three white chicks with pompadours pecked the grass. Ah, there was that strutting *gallo*. As if on cue, he jumped on a boulder and began his morning song. Funny—he sounded much better when I wasn't trying to sleep.

I grabbed something to eat and crawled into the van. Six of us bumped along the potholed road to the gated community of Los Reyes, where we picked up Winnie, an eighty-year-old ex-pat and birder, who'd spotted over 600 species in her years in Costa Rica. A right turn at a church led to a dirt road, and off we straggled, binoculars *en neck*, hoping to spy on the *aves*. Don't let anybody fool you—birdwatching is an *extreme* sport. You need strong neck muscles to stare up at trees, and the stamina of a decathlete to stand unmoving for long blocks of time, waiting. Something moved, but what was it? Something screeched—my comrade tagged it, "pissed-off-bird-in-tree." We saw one. It was identified: "fat-bird-sitting-on-rock." Perhaps our attitudes needed adjusting.

I walked ahead and noticed the towering Guanacoste tree backlit by the early morning sun, and I felt as if I were in nature's cathedral. I touched the velvet leaves of an unknown plant and peered through my binoculars at a tiny blue flower, likely a weed, that wowed me. A yellow-breasted tropical king bird perched on a bare branch, impossible to miss in all its glory. Kikskadees warbled their dawn song. And back at the van, we picked up the peach-orange blossoms of the magnificent *flor de bosque*, flower of the jungle, for keepsakes.

When others complimented my waking up early, trekking out ahead, and evident enthusiasm for the flora and fauna of Costa Rica, I started to dismiss them. I began to answer back and say, "Come on, does anyone really change and how do you think I'm going to act when I returned to San Francisco?" ... but I stopped myself from going there.

I had to rise early once more. This time it was 4:30 a.m. and I was going home. The wind had stopped, the rooster was still alive, and I had been on a daring adventure. A visit to the psychiatrist forestalled—further travel prescribed.

Stravinsky's Gift

Laurie McAndish King

Stravinsky stretches languidly, neck to toe, then falls onto his butt. With only one useful leg and no tail feathers to speak of, his balance is compromised. He cannot perch. He is forced to live on the floor of his cage, hopping on one foot, tail feathers worn to nubs. The flight feathers on each glossy green wing—which should be long and elegant—are also shortened from constant rubbing against the floor. They give this small toucan the sad, stunted look of a multiple amputee.

Peering into Stravinsky's cage, I am immediately drawn to him, although I cannot say why. Perhaps I identify with his melancholy. Or maybe I know, somehow, that he has a gift for me. But Stravinsky will not make eye contact—his only acknowledgement of my presence is a nervous hop to the far side of his cage. I wish the skittish creature would reciprocate my interest.

We have come together at *Finca Fango de la Suerte*, the sprawling central Costa Rican home of Joan Hall and Lenny

Wandering in Costa Rica: Landscapes Lost and Found

Karpman, who have created a sanctuary here for more than forty injured and unwanted animals. The climate is nearly perfect, the air is clear, and the *finca* exudes a warm, amiable hospitality. Stravinsky has lived here for three years, recuperating from his wounds. I am visiting for two weeks, craving sanctuary myself.

I love the name of the place: A *finca* is a small ranch, and *fango de la suerte* translates roughly as lucky mud. It's a reference to *Cat's Cradle*, the Kurt Vonnegut, Jr. novel in which God created the earth and then woke up the mud so it could see what an excellent job he had done. "And I was some of the mud that got to sit up and look around. Lucky me, lucky mud ... I loved everything I saw!"

Joan and Lenny love everything they see, too. They have brought homeless cats, dogs, and birds to *Finca Fango de la Suerte*. The place is a tropical madhouse. Roosters crow at midnight and kittens eat butter off the breakfast table. Parrots laugh raucously and screech "Grandpa! Grandpa!" when Lenny walks by. Six dogs lick my bare feet and legs at every opportunity. Their tongues are long and soft.

But it is Stravinsky, a fiery-billed aracari, who captivates me. A riff of red across the small toucan's golden breast conjures blood, as though he'd recently lost a fight. Stravinsky won a fight, though—a fierce one. Years ago, he was attacked as a nestling by a marauding rat, which gnawed all the toes off the tiny bird's right foot after brutally devouring his sibling and nest mate in its entirety. Left alone,

Stravinsky would have starved to death—if he had not been eaten first by a snake, a coati, or another rat. But Stravinsky was saved, and brought to *Amigos de las Aves*, a rambling avian rescue center founded by Richard and Margot Frisius on the slopes of the Costa Rican rainforest. In the wild, small flocks of fiery-billed aracaris forage for fruit and insects in the humid forests. As many as five adults sleep together in old woodpecker holes—tails folded over their backs—and share parenting responsibilities. At *Amigos de las Aves*, the parenting responsibilities fell to Richard and Margot. Their witty name for the bird—Stravinsky—was a nod to the great composer's *Firebird*.

Maybe it was more than a nod. Stravinsky-the-composer was evolution in action: restless, curious, experimental, moving listeners through chaos to complexity. His intention for *The Rite of Spring*, for example, was to produce a "bloodcurdling" masterpiece evoking the unsentimental savagery of the natural world. *Firebird* is uncharacteristically melodic, a respite from Stravinsky's dissonant style, just as *Amigos de las Aves* is a respite from the realities its inhabitants faced in the wild.

Underfunded, *Amigos de las Aves* could not provide the high level of ongoing care Stravinsky required. So he moved to Lenny and Joan's *finca*. Lenny built a special cage with a high floor and an orthopedic perch. He situated it near the kitchen door, so the forlorn bird would have regular company and eye-level stimulation. Stravinsky eschewed his special perch, but gradually developed a relationship with Joan and Lenny.

Lenny introduces me to Stravinsky one morning at dawn, and I watch as the bird hops on his one good foot and balances on the stump that is his other leg. He doesn't screech like the larger birds, but chatters a quiet greeting. Lenny feeds Stravinsky a few slices of banana and fills his bowl with diced watermelon, pineapple and papaya. Stravinksy eats the banana first. It's his favorite food.

    The next day, Joan opens the cage door and shows me how she makes a game with the first two fingers of her left hand, scissoring Stravinsky's beak. He stutters softly and nudges back, caressing her fingers with his beak. Then Stravinsky licks her fingers with his slim brown tongue. Joan says he likes the salt from her skin. She tosses a single piece of kitty kibble toward Stravinsky and he catches it in mid-air. They play well together.

    That evening when all the other birds perch, both feet locked in sleep, Stravinsky slides his long, elegant bill through the bars of his cage and leans against it for support. That beak is a beauty: the upper mandible is vermillion, fading like a sunset to yellow-green, and then again to violet at the base. A crisp daffodil-colored band marks the line where bill meets face on Stravinsky's left side—his good side—but runs ragged and muddy on the right.

    I wanted to learn more about Stravinsky, so Joan and

Lenny took me to visit *Amigos de las Aves*, the eight-acre rescue center where the bird grew up. It began as the *Flor de Mayo* botanical preserve, founded by Sir Charles Lancaster, renowned naturalist and botanist to Queen Victoria. Sending exotic specimens home from the colonies was a noble scientific pursuit, and Lancaster procured thousands of plants from Central America for the Royal Botanic Gardens at Kew, which now boasts the world's largest collection of living plants.

Today *Flor de Mayo's* history is commemorated by a single, modest wrought-iron sign that uses a few weak curlicues to decorate the rusting letters of the words "*Flor de Mayo*." The dark, damp grounds are populated with tall palms, giant climbing philodendrons, and uncountable epiphytes—plants that depend on others for their physical support. Orchids hide their beauty in the dripping undergrowth.

Richard and Margot transformed the silent botanical preserve into a lively avian rescue center, *Amigos de las Aves*. The couple had relocated to Costa Rica in 1980 with their own menagerie of exotic birds, some of which they acquired when Richard worked in Africa for Pan Am. Richard built special outdoor cages for the birds, using wire screening with squares of just the right size for the birds' feet to grasp comfortably.

The couple's reputation as animal rescuers and rehabilitators grew, and now *Amigos de las Aves* is inhabited by hundreds of "donated" birds—former pets who turned out to be too noisy, too smelly or too aggressive for their owners' tastes. Parrots, macaws and other colorful exotic birds who were confiscated from poachers—presumably destined for the illegal pet trade—ended up here, too. Many of the birds at *Amigos de las Aves* can be re-released, if habitat is available. Some, like Stravinsky, cannot.

Amigos de las Aves specializes in the rescue and breeding of macaws. I saw at least two hundred there. One of the species they shelter, the great green macaw, is the second-largest parrot in the world; its wingspan is well over a meter. In the wild, great greens can live for more than fifty years. They usually fly in pairs or in small groups—unlike many birds, these have family values.

Millions of great green macaws once migrated between Honduras and Ecuador, their flight following the fruiting of the *almendro*, or wild almond tree. Today, ornithologists estimate there are at most 250 individuals left in the wild, and fewer than a third of those are breeding pairs. *Amigos de las Aves* is the only place that has been able to breed great greens in captivity. But successful captive breeding does not solve the problem. There is nowhere for the great green macaws to go.

Logging has destroyed most of their habitat. Seventy of *Amigos de las Aves* great greens are ready for release now, awaiting appropriate sites. They need an adequate natural food supply, nesting sites, and the guaranteed safety of a private lodge or protected reserve. In the meantime, most live in small cages, too crowded to mate. Overcrowding makes them cranky. The longer the macaws are here, the more difficult it will be for them to find food in the wild, to build nests, reproduce and avoid predation. The staff and volunteers at *Amigos de las Aves* are searching for release sites.

The visit left me discouraged, but Joan was philosophical. "The macaws are not destined to live on this earth for very long," she said.

The next morning, Lenny feeds Stravinsky his fruit. Stravinksy begins eating the banana, but when Lenny moves on too quickly to feed the other birds, Stravinsky stops eating and bangs the bars of his cage with his beak in protest. Lenny returns and rubs Stravinsky's outstretched bill with one finger, petting the top of his tiny head with another. They have developed a sweet ritual.

The days pass, and I continue to visit Stravinksy. I learn to stand a few feet back from the cage, so as not to frighten him. I speak quietly, tell him where I live, muse about the weather and upcoming elections. I admire the rhythmic pattern of shallow, saw-like serrations along the edge of his powerful bill; they would have been useful for feeding in the wild. In the evenings I stop by to bid Stravinsky goodnight, but he is usually already asleep.

One warm afternoon Stravinsky bathes in front of me,

balanced on one foot, his short dark wings beating like miniature outboard motors, wet belly feathers wilting in a bedraggled mess. He uses his beak to splash water out of the shallow bowl in his cage. The spray is cool, and I feel as though we were bathing together, Stravinsky and I.

Afterwards, I watch Stravinsky hobble over to his fruit bowl. He stumbles once, then continues. The little bird picks up a cube of watermelon with the very tip of his bill. In one fluid motion, he opens his beak, tosses the fleshy fruit back into his mouth, and swallows. Then he picks up a second watermelon chunk, hops back over to where I stand watching and extends his bill out through the black cage bars toward me. He is still holding the watermelon.

Is Stravinsky offering me his food—food that he cannot catch for himself, that he is dependent on Joan and Lenny to provide? If so, I am humbled by such trust and generosity. I am also perplexed: Lenny had asked me not to feed the birds, but he didn't say what to do if a bird tried to feed me. Should I accept the soft, pink piece of fruit? I am not as trusting as Stravinsky is. I back away from the gentle aracari and his powerful, serrated beak.

Stravinsky looks at me and waits, a large drop of liquid wobbling at the base of his bill. It looks like a teardrop. He balances on one leg with his good side facing me.

I look back and reconsider. The red band across Stravinsky's belly reminds me of the belt on a swashbuckling pirate. His eyes shine clear and curious, with an inky pupil polka-dotting the center of each bright white iris. That droplet on Stravinsky's beak is not a tear; it is juice from the watermelon. I step closer and smile at the plucky bird. He had a rough start, but life is good here in the land of lucky mud.

Lenny walks over to the cage, sticks his finger in, and strokes the bird's back. Contented, Stravinsky closes his eyes and purrs.

The fiery-billed aracari (*Pteroglossus frantzii*) breeds only on the Pacific slopes of southern Costa Rica and western Panama. The great green macaw (*Ara ambigua*) is also called Buffon's macaw. Learn more about *Amigos de las Aves* at www.hatchedtoflyfree.org.

Terror in Escazú

Carol McCool

The large home in an affluent gated community disguised the danger within. I had agreed to help my friend, Mike, by running his bed and breakfast while he was out of the country. At first glance the place, decorated with bright textiles, framed charts of the fish in Costa Rica's waters, and a collection of wooden masks from local indigenous tribes, exuded a homey feel. But by evening the masks evoked an eerie, unsettling mood; their grotesquely carved faces seemed to glare down from the dining room walls.

Mike had displayed live parrots and boa constrictors in the past. Most recently his décor featured a ten-foot snake that had been captured on the patio and imprisoned in a huge glass and wood terrarium—until it vomited a partly digested rat. Suddenly believing the snake was bringing bad karma, Mike released it to the river bank outside the back patio wall.

On the patio, an enclosed habitat held two white-faced monkeys, Lucy and Suzi. Guests loved to watch the coy antics of these nimble creatures about the size of housecats. Mike's four small dogs ran around the enclosure and sometimes barked at the monkeys.

Those dogs must have driven the monkeys mad. On the second day of my stay, a mishap with the cage door at feeding time gave them the chance to lunge through the opening. They leaped upon me and sank their fangs deep into my flesh. My screams mixed with their blood-lust shrieks. A guest raced to my aid and pulled one of the raging carnivores from me. It immediately pounced upon one of the dogs; the dog howled in agony. More guests rushed to my aid and freed me from the attack.

As we all dashed for refuge behind a closed door, I grabbed the whimpering dog with one hand and a towel with the other. I hoped to stop the blood gushing from the wounds in my leg, chest and hands.

I expected the monkeys to escape by leaping to the rooftops and trees, and then to the canyon and river below. But no. More than freedom, they sought revenge. Screeching with defiance, they bounded into the kitchen to swing on the cupboard doors. Suzi pooped on top of the refrigerator while Lucy ripped open a box of pancake mix and flung its contents around the floor. Their eyes crazed with power, they defied anyone to try to stop them.

One of the guests in our huddled mass slid a cell phone and a business card from his jacket pocket. With a shaking hand, he punched in the number of our only hope. He had met her a week earlier at a wildlife conservation forum.

Who can tell how much time passes while waiting for deliverance? Finally, we heard the unlocked front door open and knew that Jackie, the Monkey Whisperer, had answered our prayers.

With a confident voice she told us to stay quiet, as she strode toward the simian miscreants. Curiosity overcame our fear, and we opened the door a crack to peek through.

The Monkey Whisperer was a tall, strong woman with flowing blond hair. She wore khaki shorts, tan leather boots and a flimsy white blouse that barely contained her voluptuous shape—the perfect Jane for a Tarzan movie.

As Jackie entered the kitchen, her resolute presence slowed the rampage. She uttered soft sounds and the monkeys stifled their shrieks.

Who is this? They seemed to wonder.

The Whisperer mimicked the monkeys' head-tilting and murmured more soothing sounds. Puzzled expressions on Lucy's and Suzi's faces told us the magic was beginning to work.

Inching closer, then bounding out of reach, they seemed to be telling themselves, *I want to hear what she is saying— no, keep your distance!*

Lucy screeched and threw glassware onto the floor when Suzi got close to the stranger.

Jackie ignored Lucy and patiently, calmly whispered toward Suzi. Suzi exploded in a frantic race around the room, then paused and, with a nervous-looking grin, tilted her head to study the Whisperer. Eventually, Lucy joined her, and the monkeys' chirps and squeals seemed to continue the debate.

Can a human ever be trusted?
Watch out, it's a trap!
But at last, a human who understands us ...

The dance of rapprochement ended with Suzi and Lucy allowing Jackie to stroke them gently, exuding a homey feel.

With her quarry purring in her satchel, the Monkey Whisperer strode toward the door.

"Where are you taking them?" I asked.

"They are going to a zoo where they will be rehabilitated and then released into the forest."

She turned and called out over her shoulder as she disappeared down the street, "Wild animals do not make good pets."

Peaceable Kingdom

MJ Pramik

Barbara licked my lower calf. It was love at first sight. Hers.

Costa Ricans love life, family, neighbors, peace, food, and sweets. These themes about this most central of Central American countries blared through the library of travel books mounting on my bedstand, desk, bookcases. I was enamored of the peace-loving *Ticos* who disbanded their military in 1948. And they do love their dogs. This fact did not make the travelogue pages. It appeared as a postscript on my Costa Rican host's e-mail.

Don Lenny had offered his small rancho outside of San José for a week's writers workshop in the dry season. His five-page single-spaced missive about the assorted insects (four thousand species), hideous spiders (tarantulas), and venomous snakes (the elegantly toxic fer-de-lance) did not deter me from prompt enrollment. His description of his pet menagerie did: six dogs—"I'm a cat person," I'd say to

Wandering in Costa Rica: Landscapes Lost and Found

anyone offering me their teeth-bared pup to pet—six cats, one fiery-billed aracari (a toucan cousin), eleven parrots, and assorted chickens penned with a barrel-chested white rooster. Lenny casually noted the canine members attack a new guest with bravado and sport. Not my idea of fun since my left calf still sports the scar from a boxer bite received at age twelve. Did I mention that I'm afraid of dogs? My psyche still feels the stitches. I secretly envied my son's animal-loving DNA and his enthusiastic ability to bathe guide dogs for the blind while I waited in the car for him to finish fluffing his canine family.

Retrieving me from the Juan Santamaría International Airport at midday, Lenny delivers a greeting that reflects a perfected professor's banter about the land crossed with the full-blown love of an expat. I held on tight as we jerked through San José traffic and across Costa Rican country roads. Oh dear. My journalist's eye noted dogs on both sides of every road and sidewalk, at least one per meter. I started to multiply the land mass by one: dog density was high, way high. Dogs—medium, small, German shepherd, Doberman with ears not clipped, yapping Chihuahua—are everywhere. On the way to *Finca Fango de la Suerte*, we stop at the residence of Fleur de Liz, hairdresser to Miss Costa Rica, whose mechanic husband tunes the van we will rent for the week. Do I dare step out of the Kia SUV as three menacing Chihuahuas surrounded us? Chihuahuas aim for the throat, my Hollywood education reminds me. Fleur, dressed in black shorts and black T-shirt, welcomes us, gushing in Spanish. Via linguistic osmosis and as a guest in her country, I step out of the vehicle and pray. Surprisingly, the dogs charge and stop six inches away, barking wildly but no teeth in flesh (mine). The teeniest ones sniff my feet. *Muchas gracias, todos santos.*

When we arrive at Lenny and Joan's rancho, he honks the horn twice, a signal to the occupants. The gate clatters and lurches open. A housekeeper grasps a huge carmel-colored creature. As noted in his e-mail, Lenny's canine tribe comes bounding out of nowhere, heaving toward the car. Will the windshield shop them? Another preconception disintegrates: Costa Rica land of peace. Pray again.

"Barbara, no! Barbara, no!" barks Lenny in an 'I'm bigger than you' tone. "Gracias, Maria de Jesus," he adds. "Barbara won't bother you. She just loves people. She's sweet and well-behaved. She just loves skin," says Lenny as Barbara explores every inch of my exposed leg with her rough, slimy tongue while the other dogs bark, jump and paw my legs in unison.

Finca Fango de la Suerte is rescue pet heaven. Costa Rican expats, Lenny and Joan, have earned the reputation of "Bring Em' On" where animals are concerned. Some pikers simply follow them home. Others migrate via neighbors, friends, locals or vets.

Currently the rancho's canine consortium includes AKC-registered Barbara, chosen by our hosts because boxers have a reputation of being good with grandchildren—she's sweet tempered but has an uncontrollable urge to lick skin. "Especially the skin of people she's never met before," Lenny explains as I stand still enduring the slurps.

Sasha, a British ridgeback—a standard breed in the Central Valley—joined the compound as a puppy as well. Joan and Lenny had stopped at a festival for children. At the adopt-a-pet booth at day's end, Sasha was a leftover. Of course, they just *had* to take her home. "She's passive and sweet, will not play with the cats. Her pals are Barbara and Tutu." Lenny scratches behind Sasha's left ear. "A German shepherd attacked Sasha one day, pulling her out from under a neighbor's bed. She had eighty stitches on her left ear and side of face." Sasha sits and casts her Mona Lisa smile up at me. My fears begin to melt.

Next to arrive was Chiquita, a shorthaired fox terrier. Most representatives of this breed that I have known could be classified as "yappers." Not Chiquita; she knew better. She had lived on a palatial Costa Rican estate that housed a zoo. One day a Doberman pup joined the animals in residence. He immediately caught Chiquita in his mouth and tossed her into the air. Apparently he'd decided the expansive acreage was not large enough for two dogs. "She adapted to our family in moments," Lenny's sighs. "She loves body warmth, obeys well, and is smart."

Golden retriever Chinoa's white fluff of a pom-pom tail—a grooming gift from the ever-smiling Maria Jesus—grew from puppy to adulthood chained to a doghouse and gate at the home of a night watchman. Chinoa, an indigenous word meaning cloud, now roams the fenced acres as alpha dog, herding the animal menagerie away from the gate when visitors arrive (except for Barbara who likes to escape). Later that evening, Chinoa welcomes me by reclining at the foot of my bed as if to ensure my safety for the night.

Estrella—pronounced *es-TRAY-ya* for "star" in Spanish—is a heartbreaker. Lenny and Joan found her scrawny body wobbling down their road, a wire wrapped around her neck. After removing the wire, they shooed her away. After all, they had five dogs already. Estrella persisted. Serpent-like, she wiggled under the front gate. The size of a stick of cotton candy with the lightness of a dandelion fluff, Estrella sat quietly one morning in the dewy grass. Next-door neighbor "Crazy Isaac" had been drinking the night before and awoke to find his garbage cans overturned. Blaming local dogs, he roared out into the yard with a nine-millimeter pistol. Unfortunately, the first dog he saw was Estrella in her own yard. His bullet shattered the bone in her front left leg. Estrella now walks with a limp and wiggly tail. "She's a ray of light," Lenny says. "She'll take a running leap into the air for sheer fun." She sits on my lap every chance she gets.

Tutu, named after Archbishop Desmond Tutu of South Africa, reigns as the only male of the canine menagerie. A miniature schnauzer, Tutu replaced Joan's previous schnauzer Bo-Bo (named after Boutras Boutras-Gali) who died a year earlier. Tutu, built solid like a muscular tank, plays havoc with all animals on site. He jumps at the young cats, Popcorn and Peanut, wrapping his mouth around their heads and dragging them over the kitchen floor. When he releases them, the male, Peanut, attacks Tutu from the rear and starts the game anew. I begin to enjoy the chaos.

Lenny and Joan don't believe in puppy school training for their charges. They bless each animal with individual love and receive the same in return. I try their technique with Barbara that first night. Barbara is attempting to mount my roommate's bed, her usual resting place. I walk over and say, "No, Barbara, not tonight. There are other places to sleep."

My tone surprises me. I stroke Barbara's head. She gazes up with liquid black coffee eyes. She has to choose: her new love—or her old bed. She seems to shrug her shoulders. A sigh heaves from her barrel chest, and she steps down onto the hardwood floor, clacking her toenails over to my side of the room to lie at the foot of my bed. I fall in love at that moment.

The *Ticos* must be doing something right by their canine pets. Internet estimates figure over one million abandoned dogs roam Costa Rican streets. With much focus on exotic fauna such as scarlet and great green macaws, nesting turtles, and assorted migratory butterflies, dogs wisely blend in with the environment. At *Amigos de las Aves* and the Hatched to Fly Free program site in Alajuela, scientist Alan Taylor notes that since the stray dogs left at their doorstep have become part of the hatchery's family, macaw theft has plummeted.

On an evening, with the pups milling about rubbing against my legs, I accept a banana bit dropped into my hand by a fiery-billed aracari. Mating pairs of parrots reside in two cages on the patio that overlook the landscaped chicken yard. Any one or more of the six cats sleep intertwined amid the glassware on the shelves. The evening holds the aura of Edward Hick's painting, *Peaceable Kingdom*, depicting the lion lying down with the lamb and other assorted creatures in a tropical valley. I have stepped into the lush canvas.

I walk out for a stroll with the dogs down to the river fence. Me alone with six dogs, chatting away about the day's events. Never would I have imagined such an evening. I had become the dog whisperer.

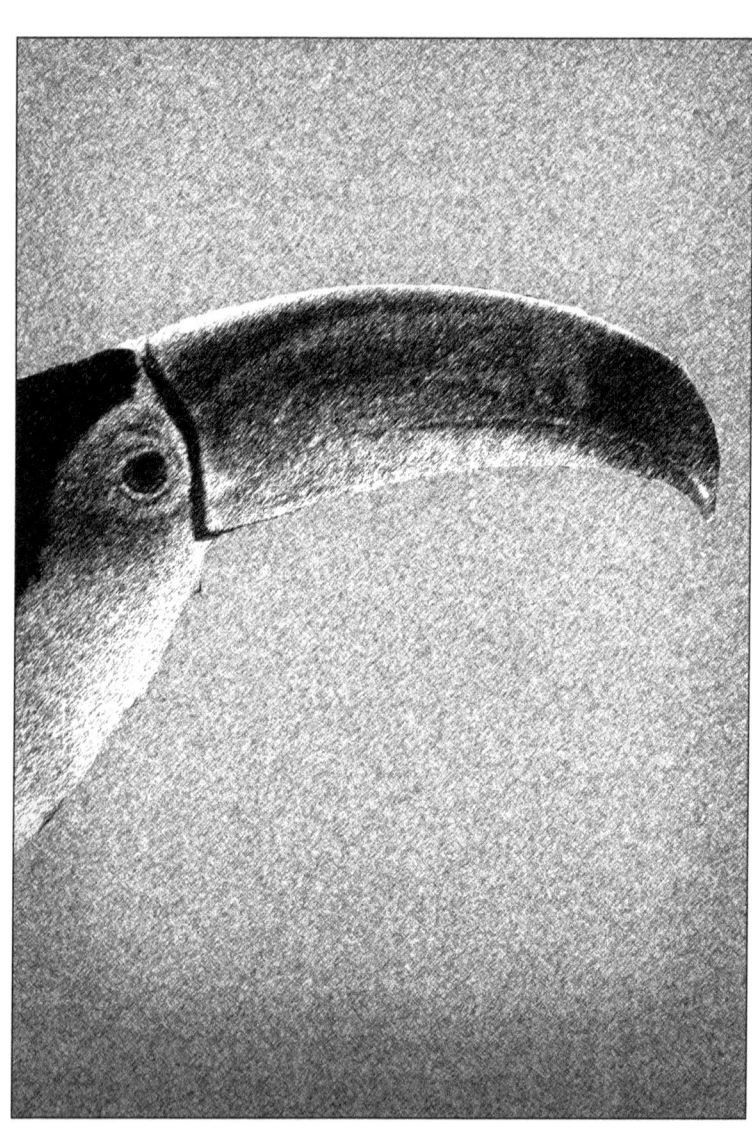

Costa Rica Animals

Thanasis Maskaleris

*Y*ou, peaceful children of this paradisiac land, you
    stare at us, visitors, with the most amiable
    glances ...
You, dogs at Lenny's and Joan's *hacienda*,
who accompany me to my morning wanderings—
you are the most devoted guides I ever had,
rejoicing in my appreciative response ...
And you, caged and uncaged birds,
you look at us, puzzled by our human gestures,
as though you want to decipher us...

   You are the barking, singing signal givers
         initiating us to your terrestrial riches ...
   You are in harmony with everything around you,
   even with us, the intruding strangers.
   Here we, wanderers with dissonant psyches,
   can attune to the harmony that Nature gives ...
   You can be our teachers of naturalness and peace,
   toward co-existence with all—with Mother Earth
         and with all of humankind ...

Ten Tiny Tico Tips for Travelers

Joanna Biggar

When traveling, it is often the small, everyday things that surprise, confound, amuse, or drive to distraction the unwary traveler. Those are also the very things that can endear one to the new culture, giving it that special *"different"* flavor. Then, with time, the strange things often become *"normal,"* that surprise of newness wears away, and in the architecture of memory become lost to larger, grander themes. But as one who believes in the power and freshness of first impressions, I wanted to record, and to share, some of my own *"tips"* on Costa Rica.

1. Road Names. Many travel guides and other accounts, written or spoken, talk about the condition of the roads in Costa Rica, a subject of such great trial to natives and visitors alike that in the recent election I understand their repair was listed close to the top of national issues. Mention the roads here, and you can set off a chain of conversation that can go

Wandering in Costa Rica: Landscapes Lost and Found

on forever, like mentioning the weather in England. But before arriving, I had no idea that once you actually get on one of these famous Costa Rican roads, you may never get off. Or at least not anywhere near where you intended to go. *Because the roads have no names.* Therefore, to find your way somewhere, you need to locate the bank, say, and turn left for so many meters, then right at a certain tree. You can see where I'm going with this. Even cab drivers get lost if they confuse one bank, one tree, for another. And you can see why just walking around a block can become an unintended challenge. Even where there are road names, such as a confusing grid of streets in the capital, San José, where numbered avenues and numbered streets intersect, the local people don't pay attention to the numbers and still want to navigate by landmarks.

2. Drink the Water, *por favor.* And While You're at It, Eat the Vegetables ... Before arriving, our preparation included the usual perusal of books, websites and health advisories, many of them plain alarming. In short, they would just casually say, *of course don't drink the water, and don't eat any vegetables or fruits, except perhaps for oranges and bananas after you have scrubbed the skin before peeling them.* The health authorities were particularly alarmist, with their prescriptions, prohibitions and maps indicating that in most of the country any visitor unprotected by full-body armor is likely to be felled by dysentery, dengue fever, malaria

or hepatitis if she doesn't die by drowning first. You have to wonder, have these people ever been here? We have drunk tap water everywhere, lived on salads and wonderful, colorful, often exotic vegetables from local markets across the country, except for the Caribbean side where we played it safe. But as for those dangerous mangoes, plantains, papayas and melons—don't get me started. REALLY, guys, if you're going to write these guidelines, you ought to get around more.

3. Christmas Season. I arrived in Costa Rica in early January, close to the mid-point of what I term an extended Christmas season, and heading toward summer. What struck me about it was that everywhere, it seemed, from private homes to businesses to the airport, there were large—sometimes life-sized—crèches. I was surprised to learn that they normally stay up until sometime in early February, and when they are taken down, it is often the time for some kind of blessing or ceremony. The time these crèches are up roughly corresponds to the long school holiday, which extends from mid-December to the first or second week of February. (Schools get two or three weeks off in July or August, which is in rainy season). By the time the crèches are put away, it is just about time for Lent to begin in the church calendar.

4. The Winds of January. When discussing the weather in Costa Rica, most guidebooks—and most people—will tell

you about the dry and wet seasons, about the oppositional moods of the Pacific and Caribbean coasts. They mention the *Vientos de Navidad*. Somewhere, once, I read that January, too, could be windy, but it a way that made me think of tea with a garrulous aunt on a lazy afternoon. Nobody mentioned that one is at risk of being blown from one side of the country to the other. Nobody warned Linda and me, when we walked the few meters from Lenny's house across the street to the neighbor's house, where we were staying, that we should dress for a hurricane. And certainly nobody said to prepare for the sounds of a shipwreck at sea while we listened all night for the house to come apart, piece by piece. Or later, when I went with my husband to Monteverde, nobody warned us that we might easily be blown out of the forest canopy, off the mountain, off the back of horses, or blown flat over.

5. Going to the Dogs. My husband is not fond of dogs, which on the face of it, would make Costa Rica an unlikely destination for him. Not that anybody ever mentioned it, but the country is overrun with dogs. They are everywhere: behind gates, in houses, in the streets. A little boy in a hairdresser's shop even thrust one in my lap, grinning from ear to ear. At Lenny's place, a pack of six ruled, and one night when I slept in the upstairs room and made it clear I did *not* intend to share the bed, I awoke to find them at the foot of the bed in semi-circle, tails wagging as they kept watch.

Which rather says it all. Despite stories of chihuahuas being chewed up by rottweilers and other terrifying dog tales, the most likely way to come to harm from Costa Rican canines is to be licked to death. Doug's assessment? "I love these guys."

6. Plugs. Ever dreamed of that distant country where you could bring appliances with their weird American wiring and plug 'em right in? Like your hair dryer, electric shaver, laptop, electric toothbrush, iPod, you name it? You plug 'em in and the fuses don't blow from wherever you are to the next continent? You say *imposible*, but I say Costa Rica.

7. Toilet Paper. Okay, from the sublime to the subter-ranean. Not parlor palaver perhaps, but still, travelers should be in the know. Costa Rica is a country that uses septic tanks, and because of same, it is the custom to use small trash cans as repositories for *papel higiénico*. There are signs in every bathroom explaining this procedure, but it still happens that foreigners can't read them, or are too freaked out to follow the instructions, whereupon they clog up the works. Which is not to discount the inherent trauma in such a cultural shift. It can even become the stuff of literature. I'm thinking here of Linda Jue's hysterical piece on her encounters with such a system in Greece (*Venturing in Greece: the Vatika Odysseys*, Traveler's Tales, 2006).

8. Natural Danger *Número Uno*. In a country beset with earthquakes, erupting volcanoes, fire, floods and sometimes hurricanes, you can imagine it could be any of these. Or, you might think, in a country crawling (literally) with poisonous snakes, its rivers filled with crocodiles, and coastal waters given to riptides and marauding sharks, there are many possible and terrifying choices. But none of these can touch, according to my impeccable source (one of our teachers at Centro Panamericano de Idiomas) the dangers of ... death by coconut. That's right. It seems that having one of those hardballs fall on your head is far more likely, and more dangerous, in this country than any of the other hazards listed above. Yup, *coconuts*. So where did you think the Marx Brothers got their start?

9. Sounds. In a visually brilliant country like Costa Rica, you sometimes have to concentrate on identifying other characteristics. But it's pretty easy to notice the sounds in a country that's buzzing, humming, barking and blowing. So close your eyes and you know you're in Costa Rica when you hear dogs barking, winds howling, sea crashing, music thrumming, traffic rumbling, horns honking, birds singing— all depending on your locale of course. But in my personal contest to choose the most telling Costa Rican sounds, I announce the winners: car alarm systems blaring endlessly and roosters crowing vociferously, everywhere, and at all times of the night or day.

10. Best Beaches. In a country with world-famous beaches, I share my two favorites. On the Pacific side, San Josecito Beach, near Drake's Bay, and accessible only by boat, is a small gem—clear blue warm water, no waves, and a curved strip of white sand fringed with a tropical forest walk, in whose trees monkeys and rare birds, including scarlet macaws and trogons may be seen. Added interest: Mel Gibson lives here, at least has a (relatively) modest house and acres of virgin forest. The house sits behind a low fence, the requisite "100 meters" beyond high tide—the Costa Rican law that determines where a public beach may become private. As for the Caribbean side, Punta Uva is also a small gem and not to be missed. That is if you don't miss it—the tiny road leading to it, seven miles south of Puerto Viejo is easy to bypass. But the small curved beach with rolling blue waves perfect for swimming also has swaths of forest along its sides and a park with snack bar, restrooms and shaded tables behind. The surf is delightful, and there are both shady and sunny spots for flopping. This beach is also notable for what it does not have: riptides, rocks, sea snakes, crocodiles and other natural hazards. I post this warning though: Both of these beaches pose the danger that those who enter their irresistible waters may never want to leave.

River Crossing

Robin Kazmier

Casey's eyes were bottomless with fear. I'd never seen anything in her dark gaze but the deep, agitated hostility that cloaked her everyday battles. Life had waged war on her from a young age, and everyone in her path inherited those battles from her absent parents. She was an 18-year-old pain in the ass who had challenged my instructions, laughed at the locals, and presumed to know everything since the day she arrived. But as the low gray clouds writhed overhead like the predatory snakes we so often encountered here, desperation overpowered Casey's defenses and pinned her cruelly in her scariest place: Trust. That's where I came in. It was certainly new territory for us, and I would have loved to reach it any time but now—on the bank of a furious river with three *Ticos* screaming across the roar for me to smack Casey's horse and send her out into the rapids. More rain was coming. We needed to cross the river, harvest as much cocoa as we could, and get back before the water started to rise.

Wandering in Costa Rica: Landscapes Lost and Found

I had been working as a volunteer coordinator on a family-owned cocoa farm in Costa Rica for probably a year. When I arrived as a volunteer myself, I had planned to stay on the farm for only four weeks before returning to the States. But Juan Luís and his family invited me to live there and organize the chaos that was born anew each day between themselves and the bizarre array of volunteers, most of whom did not speak Spanish. It sounded easy enough. Since that proposal, I had made the winding descent to this riverbank at least twice a week, convincing and then preparing volunteers to cross the river on Muñeca, a scrappy little gray mare whose name means "doll."

The vertical rows of crusty, mushroom-like growth that lined the inside of Muñeca's ears were the least of her concerns. She was the smallest of the three horses at the farm, and the only female. She didn't have the shiny coat, muscular lines or bouncy gait that the boys had. But her petite, flea-bitten body and feminine eyelashes belied a strength that neither of the others could match. She didn't snort or prance or sidestep her work, even though she was almost constantly sick. At one point the nondescript illness had taken her beyond the help of medications brought from the city, and she was pronounced "about to die." Ultimately resorting to a folk remedy, Juan Luís and two of his sons grabbed an empty beer bottle from the kitchen and filled it with their combined urine. With a single loop of rope around the base of her neck, the boys struggled to control Muñeca while Juan Luís shoved the bottle between her teeth and forced an entire bottle of piss down her throat. She protested but didn't panic. It worked; and every day since then, so had she. She was feeling fine today, ear stalagmites notwithstanding.

"I can't do this," Casey whimpered, face turning splotchy red. Her eyes begged—with a prick of accusation—for a way out.

"Okay, hang on—" I stalled. I walked back in front of the horse, tracing in my mind the exact path Juan Luís, Jorge and Chichi wanted Casey to take across the river. Often when the river was high Juan Luís would walk part of the way across it first, feeling out a few different routes with his feet, and then heaving some of the large rocks off to the side to create a safe path for the horse. But the river was far too high for that today—no human could have walked across it, and Muñeca had lost her footing more than once while taking the men across, swimming in places and dipping so sharply at one point that Jorge had nearly been thrown headfirst toward the maze of boulders downstream. We all avoided eye contact for a minute after that. Casey was next.

"This is stupid!" she shouted, tears streaming down her face now. "They're crazy! It's just fucking cocoa!"

I took a deep breath and held her gaze without moving a muscle. She was coming unglued, and the last thing I wanted to do was let on that I agreed. I was trying to silently wrestle her fear back into its place, when the pull of a familiar voice cut my stare, and I turned to face the other side.

Wandering in Costa Rica: Landscapes Lost and Found

"*¡Venga!*" Juan Luís shouted with an angry sweep of his arm, "*... la yegua ... bajo ... por allá ...*" his rapid-fire instructions drowned in the river, and I clung to the idea that dragging them up would actually help.

"*¡¿Qué?!*" I threw back at him with both hands in the air.

"*Más peligroso por ... vaya ... ¡Jale!*" (Something about "dangerous" and "let's go.") His frantic darting and pointing got the message across, and I hoped to God that the details weren't important. We were losing precious minutes before the sky let loose its rains again, and we would have no choice but to abandon the harvest and re-cross the river before we became stranded on the wrong side.

I threw my arm over Muñeca's neck and ripped my eyes away from what they were asking me to do.

"Shit!" I spat down at my rubber boots, slowly slipping down the red clay slope. I knew no one could hear me, and I begged out loud for just one more moment to figure this out. I'd spent the previous year inhabiting a little universe all my own—between two cultures, two languages, and multiple versions of what's "okay." After the first months of "in between" I had to leave my identity somewhere in the jungle just so the intense loneliness had nothing to attach itself to. I quit telling my story, quit *being* my story, and slid into the present with nothing in hand. Every action, every risk, became a deliberate act of learning, and therefore, survival. Failures, injuries and missteps sharpened me with their deadpan blade. As emotions evolved into instincts, fierce self-reliance took root where depression might once have puddled. And so I continued weighing, mediating, navigating others through the storms of cultural convergence, and occasionally, actual storms like this one. I could generally judge in an instant what version of reality I needed to guide someone through, but today my mind was slipping as much as my boots.

We were in the midst of the worst rainy season in years, and it only seemed to be picking up steam. When rumor spread that one of the two mudslides blocking in the village on either side had been cleared, we had sent the remaining short-term volunteers off to the Pacific coast through the brief opening in the road. The electricity had been out for days, the water pipes had broken under the movement of the earth, and the food supply had dwindled to almost nothing after the vegetable garden drowned. We couldn't even do the "indoor" work of shelling and grinding dried cocoa beans because the heavy dampness cultivated mold almost instantly on everything from cocoa powder to our clothes.

For weeks the river had been so high that most days we couldn't cross it to get to the cocoa orchard and continue the harvest, which was at its peak. As of the previous week, Juan Luís reported that almost half of the ripe cocoa pods were being lost to fungus and animals, simply because we couldn't get there. An un-harvested cocoa crop meant not only lost income, but also leaving the thirty-year-old trees in increased danger of being taken over—rather than pestered by—the powdery white fungus that infested the pods.

The *Ticos* were always to be trusted when we were out in the *campo*. They knew everything, and I'd already put in the time learning to trust even their most inexplicable judgment calls. But the person looking down at me from atop this haggard gray mare had terror in her eyes, and I knew that it was valid, too. It wasn't hard to imagine the tired little horse being swept away and dumping its rider into the muddy brown death trap of a river.

There was nothing more Juan Luís could do from the other side, and he gradually quieted and stared at me. I didn't know why my eye caught the boyish tufts of hair sticking out from under his baseball cap, but suddenly he snapped into focus. I recognized the man who greeted me with a huge smile the minute I got off the bus for the first time; the man who had given me my first nickname in the village, my first machete lesson, and cried when he told me about his hero, his father, over beers at the village cantina. To his left stood the man who had delicately peeled oranges for me with a three-foot machete on my first day at the farm, and months later charged to my rescue when one night I stumbled upon a five-foot fer-de-lance poised to strike, and could barely find the air in my lungs to call for help. Next to him was the young man with whom I'd spent endless afternoons hunting for medicinal plants, concocting all manner of science experiments, and bitching about the most irritating volunteers until tears drenched our laughter.

These men were not just three colorful characters in my story. They were my Costa Rican father, brother, and best friend. I was home, and I knew what they were expecting of me.

"*Vea,* okay Casey, *tranquila,*" I commanded gently.

"You're going to be fine. You're going to take the exact path Juan Luís took, okay? Now, you need to head across angled a little bit upstream, so be kind of firm with the right rein and your left leg, but give her her head. Do NOT pull on the reins. Grab her mane for support, but don't yank her head back." She seemed to be taking it in.

"You can do this, okay?" I told her firmly.

She looked across the river with doubt, but at least she wasn't crying. She stuck her feet in the stirrups and settled deep into the saddle. I laid my hands on her muddy rubber boot.

"Um, don't put your feet in the stirrups," I said quickly, and pretended to check the girth.

"Why not?"

"You just don't want to do it in a current like this; you want to have more control over your legs. Trust me."

For once, she didn't question my bullshit answer, and I never had to explain that you keep your feet out of the stirrups on a crossing like this so that if the horse falls you don't get pinned underwater or dragged downriver.

I grabbed the prickly nylon rope reins under Muñeca's chin and pushed toward the river, allowing her warm, velvety lower lip to comfort my clammy knuckles until she eased forward and we stepped into the water side by side. Our second step put us ankle deep and sent the water arcing over her hoof and my rubber boot in a slippery threat. One more step and the cool, round grip tightening around my calf told me it was time to let go. The blood in my head dropped to my suddenly cold feet as I pressed Muñeca's reins as far as I could in the right direction and released them. I let my vision fade into a daydreamy blur as Casey slowly passed by my side, and the urge to vomit tingled at the edges of my tongue. I'm no psychologist, but I know that when you're about to send an eighteen-year-old girl across a raging river on a horse she's afraid of, and you tell her she's going to be okay, you *have* to be right.

    I blinked out of the daze. No longer in the direct path of Casey's belligerence, I watched Muñeca carry her away from me with measured strides. Casey's head tilted gently forward over soft, rounded shoulders crowning a childish slouch. Her innocence stabbed back at me.

    I had heard the river's warning from half a mile away as we approached it that morning, seen it toy with Muñeca and Jorge, and I could still feel its chilling grip around my own feet. But when it grabbed hold of Casey's dangling legs and dove into her boots, I took it personally. She didn't tense up or grip the horse tighter as she descended into deeper water, and she never looked back. *If something happens to her now, there's nothing I can do. She's out of my reach.* My sudden powerlessness triggered a burning wave of rage that was perversely familiar. *If something happens, there's nothing I can do* ....

It was my father. Every time I announced my plans—my need—to venture off to Latin America alone, he exploded. As I calmly discredited his long list of absurd hypothetical disasters, his fury only grew. Of course fear can overpower reason at times—but my dad is an *accountant*.

"Idiot ..." I whispered to myself for the years I'd spent trying to overturn the fears, when all that had ever been real was the powerlessness. To which, there is nothing to say.

Muñeca staggered into the middle of the river. The water whirled tightly around her, instantly forming new swirls and eddies with sickening beauty. Casey gave up on any attempted path, and sat with motionless resignation while the river preyed on Muñeca's exhaustion, slowly pivoting her downstream and coercing her toward an area none of us was sure about. Juan Luís started to shift and pace with an ominous restlessness. He already knew about the powerlessness.

Muñeca paused for half a beat and thrust herself up out of the water with a final burst and stood dripping on the bank, head lowered, body heaving. Chichi scurried over to help Casey slide out of the saddle. As soon as her toes found the ground, she stumbled back from Muñeca, her knee-high boots filled to the brim with water. She looked up across the river with an expression like a clean slate: She was okay.

"Oh thank God," my voice whispered into the din. My shoulders and face unclenched, and I realized that I was exhausted. Muñeca was sent back across the river alone to get me, and I re-focused for my own journey through the torrent. I laced my fingers through the sparse hairs at the base of her mane, pointed her toward the water, and asked her to find her way across one more time. As we approached the deepest part, her pace slowed, and we both tensed with dread because every, single deliberate step left her teetering in the current, just barely in control. The river gushed around us, waiting for her to make a mistake. I patted her shoulder and scrutinized the flow of water downstream, mentally picking out the most immediate rocks in our path, should we stumble. But we didn't.

Muñeca delivered me gently to the other side, and I jumped down with a splash. I gave her neck a quick rub of thanks before Juan Luís snatched her reins and fiercely led her up the ridge towards the cocoa. When Chichi and Jorge turned to follow him, I put an arm around Casey's slumped shoulders and gave her a quick squeeze and a resolute glance that I hoped conveyed solidarity and evoked confidence. Relief was fleeting as we picked our way up the sloppy, copper path. The trip back across the river with the sacks of cocoa beans would likely be far worse.

Our socks squished with every step towards the cocoa orchard and the tree with all the machetes bundled in the crook of its branches. I tried to anticipate the harvest and remembered that this was also mating season for snakes. The young males would be out in droves. Good to remember, I suppose, but not something you can really prepare for.

And there on that mountain path, I got it. I got why *campesinos* act like they don't see the danger. I got why parents don't sleep at night.

Quetzal Quest

Linda Watanabe McFerrin

It was late October, the soggy tail-end of Costa Rica's "green season," a period of rainfall that stretches from May to early November. Rain hammered away at the corrugated metal roof of our bungalow at the *Fonda Vela*, an inn on the outskirts of the Monteverde Cloud Forest Preserve. Mist billowed and swirled from the floor of the valley below our balcony, erasing even the tallest trees, until nothing remained but a horizon of endless vapor.

My friend, Dixie, and I were searching for the quasi-mystical quetzal, often billed as the most beautiful bird in the world, subject of legend and song, center of Mayan mythology, national bird Guatemala—and an endangered species. Toward that end, we secured the service of Tomas Guidon, one of the best guides in the area, and with him, headed for the Monteverde Cloud Forest Preserve. During the high season, Tomas explained, the park admits as many as 400 people a day. It's not unusual to wait two to two-and-one-half hours in line. But this was the green season, a time when the riches of Costa Rica return to flora and fauna. By comparison, it was deserted.

"I don't know if we'll see a quetzal," Tomas apologized, echoing the doubts of other advisors.

Imbued with symbology—the Mayan Indians claimed that its green hood and cloak represented the lifeblood of the forest, its crimson breast the lifeblood of man—the quetzal has always been a kind of natural grail. It was once hunted and killed for the splendor of its plumage. More recently, its habitat—the rain forest and lauraceous trees that support it—has been under attack. Pesticides had killed it in El Salvador. The quetzal had all but disappeared in Guatemala. But here, in the Monteverde Cloud Forest Preserve, it was still common to see male and female quetzals, their long tail feathers streaming behind them.

Above us, the rooftop of epiphyte-laden foliage created an almost impenetrable screen from which dangled vines and lianas and the roots of other epiphytes—orchids and bromeliads. We stood on one side of a mossy gully, listening intently, blindly searching.

I do not know how Tomas saw it. Maybe he heard it first. It is partly training and partly—as I have deduced from observing less competent guides—a gift. In any event, Tomas pointed to a place in the ceiling of leaves, and while we tried vainly to see what he saw, he set up his scope, a 22x60 Bausch and Lomb Velbon; right in the center of it was the quetzal. Its plumage could only be described as lavish—crest, head, shoulders, wings and long beautiful tail a brilliant green, chest a fiery red. This bird sat patiently, turning its back to us at one point, which gave us a splendid view of its fabulous tail. Off it flew, the only quetzal that I have ever seen. We hunted for another quetzal for what seemed like hours, but perhaps a single quetzal sighting is enough for anyone. Bewitched by the rain forest, our quest dissolved under the spell of heliconia and orchids, of spangle-cheeked tanagers, emerald toucanets, three-striped warblers and slaty-backed nightingales ... under the flute-like call of the golden-browed chlorophonia.

Lost Quetzal in San Francisco

Thanasis Maskaleris

Walking on Polk Street I was stunned by the sign *Quetzal Internet* ...
You, sacred symbol of freedom, how can you be outside your
    house of Nature?
You, who stopped singing after the Spanish Conquest of your
    holy land,
    and always died in captivity—
how can you be tangled in this new maze of the Internet?
The sub-sign of the Cafe—Organic Coffee—and the
    neighboring alleys named " Willow" and "Olive"
will do nothing to make your new habitat more natural...
here where young Francisco has become a computer
    maniac...
If you were lost in this temperate city, you should at least be
in the company of birds near the statue of St. Francis, in
    Golden Gate Park—
not in this concrete wasteland where the only birds are
    greedy pigeons,
their only rhythm the "click"-adjusted head movements...

Facing Luís

Carol McCool

I do not live in paradise. In a village with a population of fewer than one hundred, we have a criminal—Luís. He served fifteen years in prison for killing two guys in a bar fight. He used a machete.

The tall, gaunt, 40-year-old *Tico* with dark, sunken eyes and a quick temper has lived with his parents since his release. They are a respected couple and owners of a large farm. Luís also spends a lot of time at the home of his girlfriend. He earns some money from odd jobs as a peon when work is available, then squanders it in bars in nearby towns. Our village in this remote mountain area of Costa Rica is too small for a bar.

Every town needs a black sheep as a warning of the dangers of giving in to temptation. Ours is no sheep. The sting of the memory of prison usually keeps him out of trouble where he lives. He does his drinking, fighting, and most drug deals elsewhere. The village returns the favor.

When passing him on the road, everyone gives him a polite greeting and keeps on walking. Yet, once or twice a year, a fellow drinker will leave a bar to run a few kilometers to warn us that Luís is in a bad state and heading our way. The neighbors call their children inside, lock the doors, close the curtains, and pretend not to be home.

As the village drug dealer, Luís became my husband's best friend. Initially, he was respectful to me when he came to our home. He even showed me the scars covering his lean torso like a hideous spider web.

My husband, Ned, had been a regular user of pot when we came here. It did not take long for Luís' merchandise to awaken Ned's demons. He quickly advanced to daily, then constant use, perhaps due to the high quality, low price and limitless supply of Colombian weed. Eventually his irrational and then psychotic behavior revealed he had progressed to more dangerous substances. During the year of hell that was our divorce, Ned was removed from our home by court order—another drama for another story.

Fernando, the carpenter who built our new house, and his wife, Daniella, lived on our property in our old house. One of Daniella's sisters is Luís' girlfriend. Luís used Fernando and Daniella as his messengers for his extortion attempt. They told me that Luís claimed he had loaned $600 to my husband before the police escorted Ned away. They were clearly worried for me as they explained, "If you do not repay the debt, Luís will damage your property. Your house has large windows, easy for Luís to break and get in. You will not be safe driving alone at night."

"That God-damn SOB!" I exploded. "Tell that liar to go to hell." A string of invectives flew from my mouth. Then my next reaction—one I am not proud of—was to counter-threaten.

"Tell him that if anything happens to me or my farm, I will be sure that double happens to his parents." Of course, I would not do that, but aggression is my immediate response to threat.

In a cooler state, I realized my threat was hollow. But I needed to stand up to him, or every other lowlife in the county would crawl out from under his rock and demand money from me for imaginary debts. My answer was an emphatic, "No way!"

I have neither weapons nor martial arts training. I am 5'3" and have not been to a gym in years. I decided to get dogs. A cocker spaniel mix had already come to live with us after leaving a nearby farm where she had been mistreated. When I decided to get more, a friend told me about a giant schnauzer that had been abandoned in a park. I rescued him and named him Oscar. The third dog, a full-sized doberman pinscher, entered my life while I was in the vet's waiting room with Oscar. The *Tico* family that owned her could no longer afford to care for her. She would have been euthanized if she had not gone home with me. Others followed, each with a story. I stopped at five.

Wandering in Costa Rica: Landscapes Lost and Found

Lest I appear braver than I really am, it should be known that that I also had the refuge of an apartment in the city. The apartment was for the Internet connection, proximity to friends and a telephone landline. My farm in the mountains has a cell phone with poor reception that requires me to walk all over a hillside to find a signal. I was not going to abandon my home there, but knowing I could flee gave me some comfort.

On my weekly trips to the city, my hands sweated and my stomach churned if I thought another vehicle was following me. For reassurance, I would reach down and touch the machete under my front seat, even though I was not skilled in its use.

Late one evening driving home to the farm I passed Luís walking on the road looking especially bitter. He spotted me and followed me with an intense glare so I would be sure to know that he knew I was on my way home. I nearly froze when I remembered that Fernando and Daniella were away for a few days visiting relatives.

I decided to turn around and make the two-hour drive back to my apartment. But first I stopped at the home of Miguel, a neighbor, to ask him if he would feed my dogs that night and in the morning.

"I'm scared," I said. "Luís knows I will be home alone. He looks awful."

"But it's too late to drive all the way back to Ciudad Colon," Miguel pointed out.

"*Tengo mucho miedo*—I am really afraid," I stammered, "I am tired but I won't be able to sleep if I stay here."

Miguel checked with his wife and then offered to spend the night on my sofa. With Miguel in the house and my doberman in the bedroom, the night passed without incident.

Luís sent more threats. Finally, I went to the police in the county seat twenty-two kilometers away. I would not back down. nor would I live in fear.

For Luís, threats seem to serve him well in the short-run for getting what he wants. I had heard of others who have thought about going to the police to report him, but I may have been the first to follow through. Even his girlfriend, whom he had severely beaten a year earlier, dropped her complaint and took him back, which deeply disappointed her family.

A young policeman listened carefully as I struggled to tell my story with my still limited Spanish. He rode with me to the courthouse and stayed with me as I made my official *denuncia*, complaint. Everyone knew of Luís. My presence created a bit of a commotion as the office staff came over to get a look at the *gringa*. I heard the court reporter use the word *mafia* and hoped it was a slang term for an opportunistic group of petty lawbreakers.

The Costa Rican justice system uses mediation, when appropriate, to try to resolve conflicts before they go to trial. A month after my complaint, a mediation was scheduled, to which I agreed. When I arrived, Luís and his girlfriend were

Wandering in Costa Rica: Landscapes Lost and Found

in the room with the mediator who did not tell me his name but launched into the business at hand. I explained I was not fluent in Spanish and asked if a friend waiting outside could join us as my interpreter. Request denied. I explained that I would understand better if they would kindly speak slowly. The other three people in the room responded by talking even more rapidly.

I expressed myself as well as I could. They called me a liar and stated that the mediation was over. I was told to leave. A total of five minutes had passed. No one would tell me what had happened.

A few days later my messengers relayed to me another communiqué from Luís. "He doesn't want any problems with you. For his part, the dispute is over. He does not want to return to prison. He will not harm you."

I struggled to understand the meaning of this surprising and welcome development, here, in a culture that is not my own. I guessed that Luís had bribed the mediator, who wanted to chalk up another success and was not concerned about the merits of the complaint. The sham mediation was intended to make everyone but me look good. Saving face is crucial to maintaining the social fabric here, especially in the rural areas. Fernando and Daniella said Luís did not want the process to go to trial, where he risked loosing his freedom—a small risk, but real. In exchange, he backed down. I wasn't sure, but it appeared I had won. For a while at least, perhaps I could live on my farm in peace.

About a year later, I was driving home in heavy rain as darkness fell. My usual route was impassable, with huge chunks of the dirt road being washed down the mountain by rockslides. I tried a longer, alternate route that was slowly filling with deep mud, which flowed like lava from another part of the mountain. Halfway through, my car was in too deep to go farther. Even four-wheel drive could not propel me through the muck. Hidden rocks could rip up my car's undercarriage. My mind searched for a way out. *Can I back up and turn around and get to a friend's house for the night? Will someone with a truck come along and push me through to a firm surface? If I put on knee-high boots and walk to safety, will my car be okay here till morning?* Sometimes entire trees and boulders the size of Buicks slide down onto the roadway here.

Then I saw a man walking toward me. *Will he help?* I wondered.

As he drew closer, I saw it was Luís, looking worse than I had ever seen him, wearing a soaked denim jacket, no umbrella nor raincoat, slogging through mud up to the calves of his boots, wet hair plastered to his head. He recognized me, and his face froze in an expression of hatred. He came closer and then began to cross the road in front of me. He bent down and came up with a huge rock, raised his arm, and leaned back to heave it at my windshield. I wondered why I was not shaking and did not feel fear. Our eyes locked. My hands still on the steering wheel, I glared back at him and did not move.

Luís dropped the rock. He pointed to his chest, then to his eye, then to me—a nonverbal threat—"I am watching you."

Big deal, I thought. *You got nothing.*

Then he continued on his way. I was able to slowly back out of the mud and get to the home of a friend and wait for the road to be cleared.

Our village still has its criminal, but now we understand each other.

Dodging Snakes in Costa Rica

Anne Sigmon

She had to mention the snakes.

"The fer-de-lance is the worst," my friend Linda pronounced as we made plans to meet on an upcoming trip to Costa Rica. She'd arranged for us to stay for several days with an expat friend of hers near San José. Then I'd head off for five days alone in a remote rainforest lodge on the Golfo Dulce across from the Osa Peninsula—the first time I'd ventured solo to such a rugged and isolated place. I am no stranger to threatening environments. I've traveled in the wild for years with my husband, Jack, a seasoned adventurer, first to Borneo taking tea with a tribe of erstwhile headhunters, later on an elephant safari in Thailand, and then on a jungle trek as the guests of a stone-age tribe in Papua New Guinea. But shortly after New Guinea, at 48 years old, I suffered a stroke caused by an autoimmune disease that turns my blood to sludge. To prevent another stroke I'd have to take dangerously high levels of blood thinner for the rest of my life.

Since my stroke, Jack and I continued to travel: to Botswana and Burma, to India, and to Silk Road cities near the border of Afghanistan. Costa Rica seemed tame by comparison: a middle-income country only two time zones away, with a stable government and robust tourist infrastructure, a "rich coast" where rainforests resplendent with scarlet macaws and a thousand species of orchids meet Arcadian, white-pebble beaches.

I hadn't considered the snakes. I also had not considered that, on my impetuous jaunt to the rainforest, I'd be alone with the only medical help a half-day slog away by boat, then jeep, then aging single-engine Cessna.

I lowered my chin and eyed Linda over the top of my glasses. "I don't plan to see any snakes." My approach to snakes, as to all other terrors, was strictly see-no-evil.

"Oh, if you hang around me, we'll see them," she said with a malicious grin. "I'm a regular snake magnet."

A snake magnet? At 5'2" and maybe 100 pounds I'd never imagined her the Indiana Jones type. I didn't know where to put myself on the Indy scale: I flunked 7th grade jump rope, had to take remedial swimming to graduate from college, and still considered jazzercise a competitive sport. Then, improbably, I'd married Jack and tagged along with him to some of the most rugged spots on earth.

"The fer-de-lance can kill you in minutes, you know." My

conversation with Linda was turning into a scare-fest. "Stealthy little things, too."

A vision of slithering malevolence wriggled across my brain. I tossed my head to shake off the dread. Just what I needed, something else that could kill me. I had already had plenty to give me the willies: a pesky infected finger that was threatening to go septic, the specter of tripping over a tree root, or a coconut falling on my head.

Since the stroke, my doctor always blanched when I planned these escapades, but he didn't forbid them. Costa Rica didn't seem to bother him. "Just don't get an infection, don't fall down, and *whatever you do, don't hit your head*." A few months before I signed up for Costa Rica, I'd been laid up for five weeks after a spontaneous bleed flooded my knee joint, a predicament that at its worst could have resulted in the loss of an appendage. The doc didn't have to spell out what would happen if super-thinned blood leaked into my brain.

A mere three weeks after our snaky conversation, I was in Costa Rica lurching along in our host's rattletrap van with its cracked windshield and balky door, through the gates and onto the grounds of the *finca* where we would spend the next few days. As the gate rolled open, we were greeted by a cacophony of yapping dogs, squawking parrots, and a one-legged Toucan named Stravinsky—a small part, our host told us, of his menagerie of rescue animals. He said nothing about snakes. *Good sign.*

Wandering in Costa Rica: Landscapes Lost and Found

 Bamboo wind chimes clacked like a marimba in the breeze as our host led me and two other guests on a tour through the Japanese Zen garden, past a koi pond, out to the four-acre tract where poinsettias bloomed big as a trees alongside birds of paradise and pink ginger. My mind raced ahead to an afternoon lolling on the grass, reading and getting lost in this Shangri-La.
 Linda joined us in the garden a few minutes later, her smile bright with mischief. "Did he tell you he had a fer-de-lance here? Right here, in the garden?" I wasn't falling for that. No way. I looked over at our host.
 "It's true," he said with the nonchalance due the sighting of a gopher. "He slithered right over my wife's foot. She was wearing sandals."
 Over the next knoll, he pointed out the copse of thorny bushes he'd planted to keep his dogs away from a nest of boa constrictors.
 "Boa constrictors?" I gulped.
 "At least six of them. One tried to climb into the aviary and the gardener had to shoot him."
 I decided to skip the garden and spend my afternoon reading by the pool.

Later, while Linda and others in our group sipped Chilean chardonnay on the veranda, my eyes were glued to my computer, surfing the net. I learned that Costa Rica is home to 135 species of snakes, seventeen of them poisonous.

Each year, more than 500 unfortunates are bitten by these venomous reptiles; ten of them die. *Less than two percent— pretty good odds*, I thought. *Unless you're one of the ten.* The majority of fatalities occur in remote lowlands without immediate access to medical help. I was pretty sure this applied to my isolated eco-lodge.

I also learned that most poisonous snake bites in Costa Rica come from the fearsome fer-de-lance, known locally as the *terciopelo*, Spanish for velvet, "one of the scariest snakes on the planet," according to an Internet rack-up of the world's deadliest snakes. Most active at night, these snakes typically hide among tree roots and leaf litter during the day. *Terciopelo* earned a "danger quotient" of twenty-four, shared by only one other snake: the Australian taipan. Africa's feared black mamba rated only a twenty, India's king cobra an anemic nineteen.

The next day our group headed out in our jalopy van for a bone-jarring day-trip to Playa Blanca on Costa Rica's central Pacific coast, a journey our host predicted would take an hour and a half.

"There are closer beaches," he told us, "but I want one that's safe for swimming." I shot him a raised eyebrow. "It's the riptides," he said in answer to my unspoken question. "They're fierce. It's terrible how many people are killed by the undertows." *If the snakes don't get me, there are always the riptides.* To rate my swimming skills poor would be an egregious overstatement, and this trip I wouldn't have Jack to hang onto. *Better just stick to wading*, I told myself.

I braced myself against the ceiling as our van pitched and jerked over the pot-holed mountain road, relieved that I'd snagged one of only three functioning seatbelts. From my rear-facing seat I had a perfect view of our crew: eight mostly middle-aged women and one octogenarian man squashed together on bench seats, laughing. They bobbed and weaved in unison as the van swerved, then popped up like jack-in-the-box puppets every time we hit a pothole. I tightened my seatbelt. One good bonk could send me careening straight into a blood-thinning debacle.

About an hour into the trip we stopped to photograph a float of snarling crocodiles sprawled on the bank of the Tárcoles River, buffeted by a gale that threatened to sweep us directly into their jaws.

"Never underestimate them," an expat member of our group told me. "People around here get killed all the time." I shivered at the seemingly endless opportunities for oblivion.

Back at the van our host offered coffee, but I asked for a ginger ale instead to calm my stomach, gippy from riding in the backward-facing seat. "Why don't you change with Linda? You might be more comfortable." Linda and two others were squashed in the very back looking decidedly uncomfy to me. I shook my head no. No way I was going to give up that seatbelt.

As the van chugged up the mountain, I was lulled into a

doze. I jerked awake as we swerved to miss, what?—a dog? a boulder? I didn't see. We all flopped to the right; I clutched the roof handle until my fingers went numb. Just as the van leveled off, before any of us could giggle in relief, we were slammed by a ferocious jolt and the sickening sound of metal scraping concrete. My seatbelt dug into my queasy gut; I braced one hand on the ceiling and two feet on the floor while my van mates flopped forward and back, side-to-side. In an eerie second of silence, I saw one chin hit knees, a shoulder rammed into window glass. What I didn't see was Linda, short and seated in the back row where the van's springs were shot, catapulted straight up into the roof.

"Oh, sorry, sorry, damn unmarked *tope*," our host swore as he pulled over to the side of the road and stopped, pointing to the camouflaged speed bump. "Everybody okay?"

"Okay, here," one chimed. "Only lost two marbles," another joked. But the banter was cut short by a low tremulous moan coming from the back seat. Linda sat up slowly, holding the left side of her head. She looked dazed, pale and shaky. "My head; I hit my head." She wasn't joking.

Someone grabbed an ice pack from the cooler while our host, a retired cardiologist, checked Linda's head, her eyes, her pulse. The rest of us stood in a semicircle shifting nervously, barely breathing. After a tense couple of minutes, he smiled. "You'll probably have a nasty bump tomorrow, but I don't think it's anything serious." He chased the rest

Wandering in Costa Rica: Landscapes Lost and Found

of us off to the beach while Linda stretched out in the van, better now, but still clutching the ice to her head. As I picked my way down the rutted path, carefully sidestepping the gnarly roots that looked an awful lot like snakes, I shivered to think where we'd be—where I'd be—if I'd been the one to crack my head. *Good lord, what have I gotten myself into? I thought this was the safe part of the trip!*

By the end of the week, despite Linda's predictions, I hadn't yet seen a single snake—not at the *finca* or on the wooded path to the beach, not on our walks to town or our visits to a forested macaw rescue center. But everyone—*everyone*—I'd talked to said, there's no getting around it: when you go to the jungle, you'll see snakes for sure.

What was I thinking? I fretted to myself the night before I hopped a single-engine Cessna for my flight to the isolated Golfo Dulce. *What was I trying to prove going to a place like this alone?* Traveling with Jack, I felt protected if not exactly by *him*, then by his good-luck juju. Jack wasn't afraid of any-thing, and his fearlessness rubbed off on me. Nothing bad ever happened with him around.

And if—or more likely, when—I saw a snake, what then? Would I watch with fascination, maybe even take a picture? Or would I run screaming down the trail, ruining the hike for anyone else around? If I heard that a fer-de-lance had been spotted near the lodge, would I don my tennis shoes and carefully make my way to dinner? Or would I hide out in my cabin eating power bars for the next three days?

Approaching Playa Nicuesa by boat, the indigo ocean melts to aquamarine in the shallows where the forest-green canopy spills unimpeded into the sea. The lodge and guest cabins are invisible from the shore tucked into a dense jungle of ceiba and cedar, cacao and mango. I followed Jody, the guest coordinator, along a winding path through a botanical garden lush with blooming hibiscus, heliconia and flaming ginger.

"There are just a few rules," she said. "Always wear closed shoes in the jungle—*no sandals*—and be in off the trail by five."

"Because?"

"Everything's more active at night. Especially the vipers."

"Oh."

After lunch, I met my guide, Vladimir—a *Tico* with possible Russian heritage—for my first jungle hike. Following him into the forest, I felt like I'd stumbled onto an action movie set: Vladimir the hero with his shaved head and pumped triceps, brandishing a machete to hack anything that blocked our path. My skin was damp in the afternoon heat. As we moved deeper into the woods, speckles of lacy sunlight filtered through the forest canopy. My ears buzzed with the mad sawing of cicadas and a whimbrel's high-pitched cry. The carpet of dry leaves crackled as we ambled forward. At least the snakes could hear us coming.

"What about snakes?" I asked Vladimir.

"Oh, they're here."

"Will we see one?"

"We might. Just watch where you step."

Up ahead, a mish-mash of tree roots and dead leaves obscured the trail. I shivered in the heat.

"If I see a snake, what should I do?"

"Just stand very still and let it pass. Don't approach it, and don't run."

I practically tiptoed around tree roots and over streamlets, praying for the steel to stand my ground. A deep, menacing growl exploded from somewhere above—howler monkeys. Following the sound of the Kong-size roar, I looked up just in time to see a dark blotch hurling through the tress. Suddenly, Vladimir stopped, signaling "sshhh," pointing down toward a copse of bushy fern. I stood frozen, listening, for three seconds, maybe four as the howling receded in distance. A rustle sent my heart pounding. I darted back down the trail— so much for standing my ground —then laughed when I saw the object of my terror: a tiny neon blue frog. "A poison dart," Vladimir said. Poisonous, what else?

Over the next few days, I didn't worry so much about snakes. There was too much else to enjoy: tiny translucent crabs scurrying across the sand, dolphins who played racing games with our boat, a coati napping in a tree trunk, a mischievous spider monkey who nabbed the pen out of my hand. I kayaked through a mango grove and sampled the fruit of a cacao pod.

On my last night, I lingered after dinner in the lodge's

open-air library where a section of oversized botanical books on the bottom shelf caught my eye. Bending low, I flipped through a couple of volumes, then sat on a stool to browse the rows of field guides, books on Costa Rican history, ecotravel, a travelers Literary Guide—even a Nancy Drew, *The Scarlet Macaw Scandal*. I chuckled out loud at that one. As my laugh reverberated through empty space, I realized I was alone; all the other guests and staff had returned to their cabins. The peaceful lodge turned spooky as the pulsating jungle night sounds closed in around me. When I stood up to leave, the image of a black-on-gray, diamond-patterned coil flicked off the corner my peripheral vision. My pulse raced as I hopped back from the bookcase, trying to get away from the snake. It was an automatic, almost autonomic reaction born from a primeval instinct for defense. Only there was nothing to defend against that night. It was a fer-de-lance, all right—a dead baby fer-de-lance coiled and floating in a jar of what I presume was formaldehyde.

I had finally seen my snake—just a baby in a jar, hardly a threat.

As I followed the overgrown path back to my cabin through the thrumming jungle night, I hoped I'd make it back to Playa Nicuesa one day. Maybe I'll see a real snake then.

Pepé LeCoon

Greg Bascom

Marriage is a relationship in which the male, for the sake of love, sex or tranquility, is persuaded to engage in endeavors that he alone would have the good sense to avoid. It happened to me. Bea, my wife, convinced me to nurture a savage creature, a raccoon.

We met the raccoon in Estrella Valley on the Atlantic Coast. This fertile valley, between the Talamanca mountain range and the sea, not far from Puerto Limón, has produced export bananas for about eight decades. At the northern extreme, the valley smacks into the sheer face of a plateau, as if God stuck it there to keep the rich soil from running away, or perhaps as a vantage point to look over His work. The view is spectacular. Imagine looking down on 5,000 acres of banana plants, a carpet of tall, green, living things, their leafy arms held high, swaying in the breeze, like a vast congregation of worshipers rejoicing the mountains beyond, source of the river that nourishes them.

But it is not as pristine as it appears. There are buildings hidden beneath the canopy: scattered clusters of homes for farm workers, each with a soccer field and school; packing plants with huge tubs of water to clean the green bananas before they are packed into forty-pound cartons; offices with paperwork; a noisy, greasy maintenance shop; commissaries and a Chinese restaurant; little farm *bodegas* and a big central warehouse; a central plaza for important gatherings. Small planes rise off the airstrip and fly low over the plantation, spraying chemicals to control the airborne spoors that lust to devastate the crop.

The plantation is partitioned into many farms. The farm managers, the chiefs of agriculture, production, operations and engineering, and William the general manager, live on the plateau. Their homes, separated by well-kept lawns, nestle in the shade of tropical trees that have lived there eight decades or more. There is a clubhouse, soccer field and several little guesthouses for visiting dignitaries. It is a swell place to spend a three-day weekend if you are lucky enough to be invited. Bea and I were.

We shared a guesthouse with two other couples. It had a TV in the living room that we did not watch and a fully equipped kitchen that we did not use. We ate our meals at the clubhouse where we shot pool and afterwards swapped stories with the folks in the crowded bar.

On Saturday, William invited Bea and me to his home for lunch. His wife knew how to decorate a home so that it blended into the environment. The living spaces flowed into the tropical exterior through open French doors, wood stained to diminish their Frenchiness. The landscape peering inside seemed a bit jealous.

While I chatted with William, his wife and Bea went outside to look over the grounds. After a short time, Bea marched back inside, her expression turbulent, a maelstrom caught between fury and the propriety expected from a guest. She tried not to glare at William.

"That cage is too small," she blustered.

William, the general manager, stood erect, calm, expressionless, a man experienced in handling the onslaught of storms, floods and pestilence—the wrath of nature and women, too.

"That raccoon, he doesn't have enough room to turn about and scratch his butt. It's pitiful." Bea, lover of all living things except snakes, appeared on the verge of tears. "Give him to me. Let me take him home."

I gasped at the vision of a wild creature in our ten by fifteen meter backyard. I imagined having to construct a huge circular cage upheld by posts over our garden, a wire mesh tunnel, circumference a hundred feet or more, like an atom collider, so the critter could chase his ass at the speed of light.

"I can't do that," William said. "My son loves that raccoon. I'll build a bigger cage. I promise. First thing Monday morning I'll put the chief engineer on it. We'll build him a penthouse."

I sighed. That is what I like about a general manager—decisive, authoritative, convincing. Bea seemed satisfied. I figured she had bluffed, had not intended to bring that savage to our home in the affluent suburbs of San José.

The next time we visited Estrella Valley the raccoon had a new cage, about a meter wide and nearly three meters long. The raccoon seemed elated to see Bea again, as if he knew she had fought for his freedom from cramped quarters. Bea responded by falling in love. She wanted to adopt him. William smiled and shook his head.

But several months later, William's company reorganized and assigned one overall manager to replace the general managers at their three banana plantations in Costa Rica. William had to relocate and could not take the raccoon. He called Bea and said if she still wanted the beast to come take him away.

I protested. "Where will we keep the creature? What about our cats? Raccoons have claws and teeth. How will we feed it? What do we feed it? Who's going to clean the cage? Do we get the cage too? Isn't the cage too big to move? How are we going to transport that animal? It's a six-hour drive. We can't drive six hours with a raccoon in the car. What if the cops stop us? They'll arrest us for coon-napping. It's practically impossible," I sputtered.

But Bea had a plan—get the raccoon and worry about the other stuff later.

Bea, a member of the company wives' club, had flown to

Estrella on occasion when the company plane had vacant seats to take the ladies there to play mahjongg for the day. She knew the pilot. Notwithstanding that *Don* Peter, president of the company, forbade animals on the aircraft, Bea and the pilot conspired to smuggle the raccoon aboard. She borrowed a dog cage and, as excited as a barren woman adopting her first child, flew off to retrieve her charge. Already she had named him Pepé LeCoon, commemorating her beloved cartoon character, Pepé LePew.

The clandestine mission went well until they landed at Juan Santamaría International Airport. Bea hunkered down on the plane and hoped for a miracle because *Don* Peter stood on the tarmac waiting to board. He saw them unload the cage. He peered inside and gasped. Bea stepped out of the plane. Peter looked at her.

"Who else but you," he said, smiling.

Fortunately, Peter and his wife were good friends of ours. Being familiar with Bea's antics and her love for animals he could not get upset. Instead, he thought Sarah, his three-year old daughter, would delight at seeing a raccoon. Bea invited Peter to bring Sarah to our home the following Saturday morning.

Bea had arranged to borrow a large cage on legs made of wood and chicken wire that looked like it had once held a couple dozen hamsters for sale. She bought a long chain leash for Pepé and a pair of industrial strength leather gloves designed to withstand 10,000 volts. Those were for me, the handler, the raccoon walker.

Wandering in Costa Rica: Landscapes Lost and Found

Peter and Sarah arrived at an opportune time. I was holding Pepé's leash while he frolicked in the little pond at the bottom of our garden. Sarah, wide-eyed, stood next to her father. Peter crouched beside her and encouraged her to pronounce "raccoon." Enthused, Sarah ran toward the beast. Pepé, startled by the screeching child, leapt from the pool and nipped Sarah's leg.

Fortuitously, Bea had taken Pepé directly from the airport to the vet to get him inoculated for rabies and other viral diseases. The wound from the warning bite healed without recourse to a doctor, but Sarah never asked to visit Pepé again.

Bea tasked me to feed Pepé LeCoon and walk him for ten minutes or so every morning before I went to work. Pepé foraged through our little garden using the scorched earth technique. He left a trail that General Sherman would envy. After three days, not a stalk was left standing. Expanding his range, he climbed a palm, ran along the perimeter wall and headed for our weeping willow tree. Fearing he would entangle the leash in the limbs, I tugged. The collar slipped over his head.

There is nothing more ludicrous than a grown man dressed in suit, tie and 10,000 volt gloves chasing a raccoon around his backyard until the little bastard gets into the neighbor's yard. I peered over the wall and smiled. The critter was boxed in.

The houses in our neighborhood butt against one another. Pepé had scrambled over the modest wall that separates our backyard from the neighbor's, but on the far side the solid wall of a three story building blocked his path. From the perimeter wall behind the houses, there is a precipitous drop to the vacant lot below, too high for Pepé to leap, I thought. The neighbor's backyard, half the size of ours, sported a nice flat lawn with only a bougainvillea draping over part of our common wall. I figured it would be easier to catch Pepé in that confined area than in our larger, bush cluttered space. I stationed Bea at Pepé's only escape route, the section of wall not covered by bougainvillea, and asked her to shoo him back if he tried to return to our grounds.

Our neighbor's two yapping dogs were shut inside for the moment, but I imagined the lady next door would soon turn them loose to get rid of the wild animal on her property. I hustled over to ring her doorbell, hiding the leather gloves behind my back.

"I'm sorry to bother you, but our pet raccoon escaped. He's in your backyard."

Still a bit sleepy, she looked at me, then at my yellow power-tie, back at me and blinked. "You ... you have a raccoon?"

I swallowed, nodded and said, "Yes, cute little fellow. His name's Pepé LeCoon." My attempt at personalization did not appear to aid my cause.

"A raccoon, in my backyard!"

"Sure," I said, as if most everyone in the neighborhood harbored wild animals. "May I go fetch the cute little critter?" I thought that sounded better than "capture the beast."

I slipped through her patio doors while she held her dogs at bay.

Snatching Pepé, I soon learned, required cunning, clever wits. Raccoons, having untold generations of inbred instincts to avoid predators, are tricky rascals. After several minutes of chasing, I realized the difficulty of my task. I removed my suit jacket, loosened my tie, rolled up my shirtsleeves and donned the industrial strength gloves. I felt certain of eventual success. After all, Pepé had grown accustomed to humans. I fed him. For sure, he would cooperate.

I chanted in a soft voice dripping with tenderness, "Here Pepé, come to Papa, Pepé, you sweet, fuzzy little bastard."

He did not cooperate. He sat still and pretended to ignore my sneaking up behind him until I stretched my gloved hands to snatch him. Then he darted. I lunged. He scrambled under the bougainvillea. Hah! With leather gloves I rattled the thorny bush. Swish, the sneaky fuzz ball scooted between my legs.

After fifteen minutes or so, we stopped to rest. While wiping my brow, I realized Pepé was not trying to escape. He was playing with me, running me ragged. It also occurred to me that when I caught him I would have to carry him past two angry dogs, and he would likely break free to do his scorched earth thing in my neighbor's living room, then to her kitchen where he would devastate the chinaware. I called over the wall to Bea.

"Honey, get me the dog cage you used to bring this savage to our once tranquil home."

I set the cage down in the middle of our neighbor's lawn and opened its door. With luck, I could chase Pepé inside. I stepped back and prepared to make my move. Then the incredible happened. Pepé twitched his nose, sauntered into the cage and lay down. He had tired.

Bea, without admitting to any wrongdoing, seemed to acknowledge that we had engaged in an endeavor that we should have had the good sense to avoid. And a huge problem loomed. We would soon depart for a sailing cruise around the Polynesian Islands and would forfeit the cost if we cancelled. Our maid, who tolerated our cats under duress, was terrified of Pepé and refused to go near his cage. The little tyke would die of thirst, hunger and his own stench while we were away.

Bea thought of the solution. She called Charlie, our friend in Limón. Charlie owned a tract of jungle near the port that he had bought to grow tropical flowers for export. A caretaker lived on the property. Charlie agreed to take Pepé and let him run loose. The caretaker would put out food for him until he learned to forage for himself.

Some months after we set Pepé free, Charlie told us he had found Mrs. LeCoon and started a family. I wonder if somehow Pepé can tell his kids about captivity, about the nice lady who got him a bigger cage, and about the time he played catch-me-if-you-can with the lanky gringo wearing a yellow power-tie and 10,000-volt gloves.

THE KING OF CALYPSO

JOANNA BIGGAR

Walter "Gavitt" Ferguson lives in semi-darkness, but everything about him radiates light. At ninety-one, this most famous Calypso musician of Costa Rica has lost most of his sight, but the beat, humor and joy of his songs shine on with the intensity of tropical colors under the Caribbean sun. In a bright blue and pink building named *Sol y Mar*, which serves as open-air restaurant, hotel with cabins, and shop near the edge of the Cahuita National Park beach, most days "Mr. Gavitt," as he is fondly known, can be found sitting quietly. The restaurant/shop/hotel is a family business, next-door to the neat blue house where he and his wife have lived for years. He frequently eats in the restaurant, and just as frequently, locals or visitors to the park stop to chat with this most renowned of Cahuita's citizens.

And although he no longer sings, his voice is still lyrical with the sounds of his Jamaican-style English as he continues to tell the tales he has always sung: of life in this small coastal

Wandering in Costa Rica: Landscapes Lost and Found

fishing village; of working the cocoa and banana fields; of devilish women, dangerous snakes, and the wicked city of Puerto Limón to the north; and in particular, of the wily Calypsonian, who sees all and renders all he sees into snappy lyrics with an irresistible beat.

While his songs are highly original—he has been called "one of the most important and ingenious popular composers to have appeared in Costa Rica"—they also reflect time-honored traditions, old ways and rhythms, a life of poverty and song, and a slowly vanishing world. In many songs, he consciously pays homage to predecessors such as Lord Cobra, Lord Kitchner and Papa Houdini. He is also said to be "probably the last to have learned the trade through verbal contests, dueling and improvisation."

That trade, with roots in Trinidad, Tobago, Barbados and other Caribbean islands also came to Jamaica, the birth place of Ferguson's father, who as a licensed cook, had moved to Panama for work. There he married Ferguson's mother and there Ferguson was born in 1919. But when he was two, his father sought better opportunities in Costa Rica, and became a cocoa farmer in Cahuita, years before it became a town, and decades before it had roads.

Here Ferguson grew up among cocoa fields, many of which were converted to bananas when United Fruit Company arrived; here he learned the old ways; and here, very early he developed an ear for music. At age seven, he was sent by boat to Limón to go to school and live with an auntie who had the best piano in the city. It was so precious, however, that he was not allowed to touch it. He did have a good teacher from Jamaica, though, who recognized his abilities in math—which he later used to make a lot of money by figuring lengths of wood for cutting into lumber. By age eleven, he fled the auntie, whom he considered too strict, and returned to Cahuita.

At thirteen, coming back from the fields with his father, the boy was struck and bitten by the fearsome *terciopelo*, or fer de lance, Costa Rica's deadliest snake. Along with many other species, it thrives in the fields and coastal jungles of Cahuita. Although there was a French woman doctor who lived there and treated everyone, for this emergency, the family took him to a local snake doctor, who cured him with a regimen of herbs for nine days, followed by a dose of castor oil.

It's not clear how soon afterwards he became noticed for his musical ability, but he had begun to pick up instruments and play the sounds he heard around him. By fifteen, he was known as the best harmonica player around. Soon he picked up the ukulele and quickly mastered it. Then a fellow with a guitar came around and let Ferguson play it. People "were amazed," he said, that he could play it right away even though he only knew the four strings he had learned from the ukulele. He quickly added two more strings to learn the guitar.

Before becoming fully accomplished, though, he was

befriended by a field hand named Mani who also played the guitar and wanted to know if Ferguson would go to a party to play with him. Since Mani was the better player, he played lead, while Ferguson played second, thus earning him the affectionate nickname "Segundo." It is a name he has kept to this day.

His true love, however, was the clarinet. He longed to have one, but couldn't afford it. Then one day, a man he knew bought one in San José, and quickly went blind—"like I am now," he said—so couldn't play it anymore. He let Ferguson play it and buy it on time. The young musician learned it in twenty-two hours.

People were once again amazed at his abilities and knocked on his gate to hear him. "In October I got the clarinet; I played for a dance in December," he recalled, smiling.

His father warned him that clarinetists "die young from heart trouble," so he didn't want to tell his father about his ambitions to keep playing. But his mother had other fears; she told him that clarinetists die blind. By the 1950s, having encountered another clarinetist going blind, he was ready to heed her, gave away his clarinet to a fellow named Absalom, and vowed to quit playing.

Long before that, however, Segundo Ferguson had made his musical mark, playing and performing his original songs up and down the coast. He played in little bands, including one of his own called "Grupo Miserable." In addition to all the instruments, he also sang the songs he had created. "My mother was a great singer," he declared. "She said I took it from she."

Because during his decades of performing Ferguson only recorded his work on home-made cassettes he gave away, it would now be all gone had not Jazmin Ross and Luciano Capelli of Papaya Music come from San José in 2002 and 2003 to Cahuita to coax Ferguson, then in his 80s, out of retirement to make two CDs. The beautifully illustrated covers, featuring pictures of Ferguson as well as the vivid colors of Cahuita and photos of the great green jungle of the national park, now contain his clear voice, his guitar, and all that there is of his life's work.

Inside the covers of *Babylon* and *Dr. Bombodee* are many worlds. Some are tributes to the long-gone days of childhood, such as "Callaloo," a local plant used to cure a variety of aches and pains, whose virtues Ferguson extols:

> Good for your belly and good for your back
> Tighten every joint that is getting slack
> I say callaloo, everybody loves
> Callaloo.

Even in those songs about childhood, Ferguson's great sense of humor shines through. In "72 Weeds," an homage to traditional Jamaican music, more plants appear, but here he encounters a woman hawking a basket full of "weeds" with ridiculous names, which, when stirred together properly, have healing properties:

> She had the Man Piaba, Woman Piaba,
> Tom Tom, Calabash, Lemon Grass
> Mini Root, Gullie Root, Racam Tu Ry,
> Madan Fate and Duppy Baty
> Yes, the woman must have been gifted,
> She was bawling out all the time.

Often, however, he is the fool or unwitting victim in his songs, as in "River Bank," a reflection on his less-than-sterling student days:

> My teacher never liked me
> The fellow said that I'm a black-headed mule ...
>
> No time at all that we could agree
> He said I'm a dunce and a bloody fool ...

In "Babylon," which is a slang term used by ganja dealers for cops, the situation is more serious when he wanders into some drug lord's territory in Limón and is mistaken for being a Babylon.

One day I was passing through the baños
I met an outraging ganja man
The fellow was so cantankerous
I thought he would have killed the
Calypsonian.

Now he started to question me
I was humble as a lamb
He wanted to know my pedigree
And where I am from.

Hear him bawling
What are you doing in here
Yes you Babylon
What are you doing in here
If you are coming to interfere
I'm going to tear off your pants
And your underwear.

Through song, too, Ferguson pokes gentle fun at the absurdities he sees around him. In "Cabin in the Wata," he declares tongue-in-cheek how "the modern generation every day/the people getting smarter," then goes on to describe how this "smart" fellow ended up building his cabin in the water.

In "National Park," he lays out a bureaucratic nightmare anyone could relate to: When the government declared

Wandering in Costa Rica: Landscapes Lost and Found

Cahuita to be a national park, residents had to fill out reams of paperwork including marital questions about their grandparents and their religious affiliation. The absurd goes even further in "Computer," which he calls a "wicked talking parrot." In this musical version of an actual event, a bunch of bureaucrats come to question a small remittance he had from his father's cocoa farm. But,

> the computer tell them this
> the computer tell them that
> and the officials they all agree
>   computer tell them
>   the devil knows what
> and they take the pension from me.

Ferguson has been married to his wife Julia for sixty-six years; together they had ten children and many grandchildren and great-grandchildren. He is also a devout member of the Jehovah's Witnesses Church whose creed excludes drink, drugs, and womanizing. Nonetheless, his songs tell plaintively of wicked women who prey on poor musicians. In "Glamour Gal," "One Pant Man," and "Carolyne," to name a few, hapless musicians fall victim to young and scheming gals, after their money or their lives (Carolyne is a necromancer). Ferguson claims the only autobiographical song among these is "Serenade," in which a young woman tries to seduce him, but the virtuous

Calypsonian sends her away with "Young gal, leave me bachelor room/Young gal, I'm begging you to leave me ..."

With blindness making travel very difficult, Ferguson declined to go to San José to make his CD's, so San José came to him. In order to record, the producers from Papaya Music had to fashion a studio from a *Sol y Mar* rental cabin by stuffing it with mattresses, unplugging the appliances, and trying to reroute tourist buses, to cut down on the background noise. The parrots and dogs were harder to control.

Now, years later, noise and activity are rampant on the main (paved) street of Cahuita. Dogs, parrots and howler monkeys continue to have their say, as do buses, tourists, surfers, vendors, Rasta men, ganja men, and on Saturday nights, dueling calypso bands up the street. But down at the *Sol y Mar*, Mr. Gavitt Segundo Ferguson is likely to be sitting quietly and smiling. For he knows what everyone in town knows: Here resides its true treasure. As he told it in "Master of Calypso":

> The people would like to know
> Who the king of the Calypso
>
> The public would like to know
> Who the king of the Calypso

Segundo is my name
Anywhere I go
I must hold the fame

They call me the hero
The killer
The *cancarra* ...

Young gal take my advice
When you get a good man to treat him nice
Treat him loving
Treat him kind
For a good man is hard to find

Take it from me
They call me the king of melody
Bam bam de ole.

Cocooning in Costa Rica

Linda Watnabe McFerrin

"The plane, Boss, the plane!"

My friend, Dixie, and I expected to see the diminutive fiqure of Herve Villechaize (Tattoo) rushing out to greet us, as a tanned and widely smiling Ricardo Montalban waited, arms crossed, in the shade of a cecropia tree.

After days of bouncing along on washed-out roads and trekking through jungle, we had finally arrived at our last stop—Lapa Ríos, a rainforest resort on the Osa Peninsula at the steamy, southwestern tip of Costa Rica. To us, Lapa Ríos, which means "rivers of scarlet macaws," seemed like paradise.

Dixie and I were traveling during the tail-end of Costa Rica's "green season," as the rainy period that stretches from April to early November is rather euphemistically called, and we were trying hard not to "cocoon." In eco-sensitive travel circles "to cocoon" is a cardinal sin. It means that you require protective bubbles of amenities like telephones and air conditioning that insulate you from your surroundings. It is counted the reason that enormous hotels like the Tambor Beach Resort, a tourist development on the west coast of Costa Rica, get built, changing the wholesome, precariously balanced ecologies of a beautiful country and generally not for the better. Resident environmentalists and adventure travel experts snarl the term. Why come to Costa Rica? Why not hang out at any Ritz Carlton or Omni Hotel at home?

So, Dixie and I had slogged through rain-soaked jungle and bounced over rutted, kidney-damaging roads, eschewing tours and overdeveloped beaches as a matter of principle. By the time the twin-engine Travel Air plane deposited us at an airstrip a few miles from Golfito, a ragged banana port on the lip of the Golfo Dulce, and we pressed our way onto a boat that was headed for Puerto Jiménez on the other side of the Gulf, we were exhausted and over-stimulated. At that point, Dixie, my travel companion and fellow material girl, finally balked.

"You know, adventure travel is one thing," she said testily over the head of a mother with a sleeping child in her arms, "but I'm getting kind of tired of feeling grungy."

It was a warning. I was, after all, the one who had masterminded our trip. It was I who'd selected Lapa Ríos as the final point of our journey.

"This," she was saying, "had better be good."

I could hardly blame her. She had already piloted a four-wheel-drive vehicle over roads that would have defied Evel Knievel, rescued stranded commuters when their bus got stuck in the mud, faced flat tires and distrustful rent-a-car people and gone without dinner in favor of night hikes on stormy trails. As we sat on the crowded, rattletrap ferry, there in the armpit of Costa Rica, I suspected she was at the end of her rope.

It was not Herve Villechaize who greeted us when we disembarked at Puerto Jiménez, delapidated gateway to Lapa Ríos, nor was it a white-suited Ricardo Montalban. We were met, instead, by blond, tanned John Lewis, a retired lawyer, Minneapolis transplant and owner—along with his intrepid partner and wife Karen—of the resort. John threw our bags into the back of his pick-up truck and invited us to ride with the luggage. Dixie raised an eyebrow.

"You'll like what you see back there," John Lewis said, in response to her look.

We climbed up into the back of the truck and braced ourselves for the ride. Bouncing along miles of rough dirt roads, we juggled canteens and cameras. John stopped often to point things out, like an immature white ibis poised in a field or a rare roadside hawk sailing toward the treetops. We were traveling through acres of rainforest preserve and our minds were about to be blown.

We weren't prepared for Lapa Ríos. Set on a leafy ridge, 350 feet above the sea, the pitched palm roof of the main lodge rose on fifty-foot rafters supporting an observation deck that commanded a 360-degree view. Around the main lodge were clustered fourteen private bungalows joined by a meandering walkway that reminded us of the native vine, *escalera de mono* or "monkey's ladder." In fact, the entire complex seemed to have grown out of the rainforest rather than to have been built there. Roofed entirely in thatched suita palm, the roofs were pitched along indigenous models so that tropical downpours glanced off them. The bungalows, walled with screens that allowed the cooling breezes to drift through them, needed no air-conditioning. Showers inside were screened by curtains of foliage. Outdoor showers were warmed by the solar-heated waters. Mosquito nets tented the beds to protect guests from wandering insects. Its post and beam architecture designed to weather local earthquakes, Lapa Ríos sat perched on hillsides ablaze with heliconia (also called bird of paradise), fiery orange wands of *Canna indica* and other brilliant blossoms.

It started to sprinkle. We got out of the truck and stepped into the lodge. Rain drummed lightly on the suita palm fronds. A gentle breeze wafted in through the rattan-slatted walls. John's staff rushed up and welcomed us, offering large, fruity cocktails. Dixie and I are both fond of garish tropical drinks. I noticed the wide smile that had spread over my travel companion's face.

Breathtakingly elegant in its simplicity, Lapa Ríos seemed the most natural place in the world, but, in fact, Lapa Ríos was built with textbook idealism. Now, this was a cocoon worthy of Costa Rica, a place to relax and unwind that was totally integrated with its environment. We had arrived at our Eden.

Most magical of all, of course, is the rainforest that frames Lapa Ríos. One thousand acres of protected land, it is one of the central reasons for the resort's existence. We roamed over much of the forest under the leadership of the resort's excellent guides—Augusto, a native mystic whose knowledge of plants and their medicinal virtues was mind-boggling (he could reel off the names of the exotic flora in Latin, English, and Spanish) and Daryll, a student from Canada and an expert on birds.

In the evenings, as we sat in the candlelit glow of the lodge, where we dined in great style under the Lewis' watchful eyes, Augusto entertained us with poetry in the ancient oral tradition, composing songs, on the spot, for Dixie and me.

We did not want to leave Lapa Ríos. Somehow we got our second wind there. Dixie, whom I thought was fed-up with jungle hikes, spent the morning of our departure looking for birds. After a rugged three-hour excursion in the sauna-like heat, she came into the lodge where I was breakfasting. Perspiring and happy as a ten-year-old child, she kept pulling her t-shirt up over her sweaty face to mop it off. In this manner she circled the breakfast room and greeted her fellow guests, heedless of her appearance. They looked at her, at her beet-red checks, at her hair plastered against her forehead, and asked warily, "Well, how was the hike?"

"Oh, wonderful," Dixie, the newly emerged Costa Rican butterfly would tell one and all, with a big fat grin.

"It was just great."

Downtime

Sandra Bracken

The garden never ends. Walking through a shaded gate by a koi pond under a forty-foot ficus tree, I am surrounded by bamboo orchids, papyrus, heliconia, mariposa palms and a cluster of crotons. Next, I'm attracted to the burgundy ti plants that line one side of the driveway across from the mix of ferns and delicate yellow terrestrial orchids that line the other side. The garden continues into the distance.

I have been here only five minutes and I'm over-whelmed. It is January. My body and brain tell me it's winter. I should be cuddled up by the fire, pouring over next season's plant catalogs. I should be looking out the window across the snow, imagining what I will plant in my garden come spring. But right now I am in the Central Valley of Costa Rica, thrust into a garden that never ends, that never stops growing. I'm on overload. I like to take notes about plants in the places where I travel, but this time I don't have a notebook big enough. My traveling companions say to me, "Don't you just love all the flowers and exotic plants? Wouldn't you like to live here?" They are surprised when I answer, "No! There's so much here; it's too much. I need a winter break."

It's second nature for me to look at, to smell, to touch each plant. In the garden of the house where I am staying there are acres to explore, but I am constantly stopped dead in my tracks. I could set a chair by the ylang ylang that perfumes the air around me or near the delicious chocolate orchid. The intense colors draw me further on: the pure sky blue of the thunbergia with its velvety texture; the scarlet trunk of the lipstick palm; a line of bougainvillea in a pallette that runs from magenta to shades of pink and purple to vermillion. It is somewhat strange to see 'houseplants'— philodendron, dieffenbachia, anthurium, ginger—growing outdoors. These large, lusty examples remind me just how beautiful they can be. I am more familiar with the paler versions I try to grow indoors. The little poinsettia at home, for example, was dropping blossoms and looking quite peaked when I left. But here, the poinsettia shrub is six feet high and in full bloom. And how extravagant to grow one's own mangoes, papayas, avocados and almonds. There's even a cashew tree. What's not to love about this garden? I've barely begun to explore it. But I can't help thinking how much work it takes to keep it in such nice condition.

Later, having left the Central Valley estate where I was attending a workshop, I find myself in Santo Domingo de Heredia studying Spanish. My teacher mentions another garden and we go together to see it. The family who developed the property visualized it as "an oasis of nature in the middle of a growing city." These eight acres seem like a combination park and small arboretum with winding paths, sculptures, some outbuildings, and areas of special interest. We walk through bamboo groves and by many clusters of heliconia, also known as bird of paradise. Orchids are not in bloom in the orchid house, but those spread throughout the grounds take my breath away in their variety and color: epiphytes in variations of white, cream and magenta; terrestrials colored pale to deep orange and yellow with touches of red.

In the extensive herb garden I easily recognize the very fragrant scents of basil and mint. The brochure says that there are approximately sixty native trees here, including one in danger of extinction, the *Guayacán real*. What I like most about this garden is its desire to inform about the wide diversity of plants in Costa Rica by using labels and a written guide. Too bad I don't have more time to take it all in. We find a bench to sit, talk and enjoy ... a pile of leaves.

Suddenly I realize they must have to rake leaves all year ... all twelve months! I don't think about raking leaves after November. Maybe in some years, when they are a little late leaving the trees, during the first week of December I'll still be gathering up the last of the crunchy air-borne leftovers. Without fail I remember my childhood. The huge piles of leaves in Virginia were the raw material that could be shaped with a rake into a plan of imaginary rooms of a castle. For a few weeks I was the artist-architect of structures large and small with unlimited resources. Finally, sadly, we raked the leaves into the compost pile. That was the order of things. Fallen leaves were not thought of for another year.

I loved autumn. It signaled an annual ritual of preparing for winter, just like the animals in some of my childhood stories. The squirrels and chipmunks stored their nuts. The frogs went into hibernation. My grandfather, who was in charge of our garden, went into a sort of hibernation too; I didn't see him working outside until spring.

Except for two years in Florida, I have always lived in a temperate climate zone, where there is a large seasonal temperature change. Summers are warm to hot and humid—80 to 100 degrees F.—while winters can be very cold with occasional snowfall and temperatures varying from below freezing to 50 degrees. In other words, in gardening terms, I have always lived in Plant Hardiness Zone 7. Plants are listed under the coldest zones in which they normally can succeed, which is required information for the gardener to know when and what to plant. For me, the last day of possible frost is May 15, and I know well that no tender plants should be put in the ground before then unless protected. Born into and living within this variation of climate and plant behavior must be part of my DNA.

Possibly it's part of my daughter's too. She says that on a random day in March she feels the pull to be out of doors.

Even in the gusty winds and mud of that month, the gardening sap in her begins to rise. Having been shut out of the garden for five months, she is eager to return, to see what has survived the cold, get her hands in the soil, moving plants and putting in seedlings.

During the two years my husband and I lived in Florida, I thought all gardens there irresistibly gorgeous—in the beginning. It didn't take long to figure out that there was a price to pay for all that prettiness. The lovely jasmine whose spicy fragrance greeted everyone who entered our house, for example, seemed to grow a foot a day. I hacked it back with great regularity lest it strangle someone. One minute it was gorgeously shaped; the next it was stunted and denuded. I stayed on the alert for too much growth all year. The banana trees continually sent up new shoots. The crotons always seemed to push beyond the fence into the neighbors' property. I patrolled outside, watchful, every day. And while I tried to lie by the pool enjoying the breezes and soft swishy sounds of the palms, I couldn't relax. The fronds were turning brown and some were hanging precariously. The guilt would creep in. I knew there was work to be done. As I turned to it, I thought longingly of the only holly tree in our neighborhood that grew several blocks away, and identified with the yearning of the person who planted it. A symbol of winter, the holly looked out of place ... the way I felt.

The gardens in Costa Rica seem to have no restraints; they know only perfect conditions for growing, all months of the year. My Spanish teacher says, *"Las plantas en Costa Rica son demasiadas!"*—the plants in Costa Rica are too much. Her words have the ring of a reality check. Constant growth means constant debris, the never-ending shedding of spent blossoms and leaves. More plants mean more maintenance. It is the gardener who must show restraint here. As I walk to and from my school I peer through high iron fences into small courtyard gardens. Neat and tidy, these are modest gardens, some with only a handful of plants. But I think that they are smart gardens, that their keepers know what it takes to keep their plants healthy and looking good.

As a traveler I have the best of all worlds. I am in awe and thoroughly enjoy the exotic beauty around me. All the while I gather good ideas and get insights into the way things are done in other places. Best of all, I don't have to rake leaves in January. My little garden at home may not have the voluptuousness of the ones I have seen in Costa Rica, but it is a garden that gives me time to greet a new season well-rested, enthusiastic, and perhaps a bit smarter. I am glad to return to my relaxing cold climate and my gardening downtime.

Roots and Branches

Carol McCool

I stumbled on the worn, uneven surface of the bare rock that formed the road winding up and around the mountainside. I strained to keep up with Daniella, my much younger and more fit housekeeper. We hiked together for the exercise and were becoming friends.

"That's where I was thrown from a horse when I was four," she said. "My head hit the rock. I was unconscious for three days."

She had lived in this *campesino* village for most of her twenty-five years except for a short spell when she worked as a maid in a small hotel in the beach town of Quepos. She and her husband, Fernando, worked for my husband and me on our small farm in these mountains. He cared for their two-year-old daughter while Daniella and I hiked early in the morning.

"How did that happen?" I asked.

"I was sitting on a horse led by my uncle. It reared up and I fell off."

Wandering in Costa Rica: Landscapes Lost and Found

"Did you see a doctor?"

"No, the nearest doctor was too far away."

Further along on our climb, Daniella pointed to a hill-side covered with bushy, shiny-green coffee plants. "For years at harvest time, my sisters and I picked coffee over there when we were children. We were poor. My mother's first husband died in a train accident. Her second, my father, drank a lot. I wanted to stay in school, but we didn't have enough money. Our house was small and noisy. With five sisters, there was nowhere for me to study."

I began to wonder what it was like to live your life in layers over and over in a small space where you turn a corner and see the house where you had your first kiss or pass the nasty neighbor who poisoned your dog. Years later you and that neighbor are both still there. You grow. People change. The place is constant. The very rocks and fields sing your story.

When I came here five years ago, José was ninety-three. His father's family had been one of the first to leave Costa Rica's Central Valley to settle this area. Before he died, José told me about the jaguars and other wild animals that had lived here when he was a boy. He described going with his father by oxcart to take the annual coffee harvest to market. The trip, twenty-five kilometers each way, took nine days because of the weight—seven days to get there and two to return. They carried their food with them and slept in the open at the side of the road. These small farms have changed slowly over the years, but they remain in the same place, a place of shared history for five generations.

Look closely at the weathered fence posts, made of *guachipelin* or other hardwood. The posts grow roots and then branches after they are sunk into the earth. *Campesinos* repeatedly cut those branches for new posts. Decades later, those dead wood posts erode into gnarled, but deeply anchored sculptures. That one looks like José, ready to pick up his old guitar and softly sing a Spanish ballad of love and longing. Look at that narrow post with the fine lines in its weathered surface. Can you see Ofelia in the wood, thin and erect, gray and elegant as she graces the fence along the road? Look over there at the wooden knots and curves revealing Samuel's face in a post as solid and unbending as he was in life.

I remember the thoughts I had when I arrived—me, a foreigner who came with a husband thinking we would build a house and spend the rest of our lives here together. We chose the place because of the view and the affordability of land and construction. Two good years passed and then one bad one. Following our divorce, I alone remained.

The community welcomed and supported me, even when they might not have understood my foreign ways. I must have been a sight to them as I bounced along the dirt road in my tiny, boxy four-wheel-drive vehicle with my long, red hair flying and my little black dog sticking her head out the driver's-side window. Sometimes, just for fun, I yelled like a rodeo rider, "Yeehaw!" The *Ticos* wanted to know and learn about me, and I about them. When a family was in need, I often helped. They called me *Doña* Carol, a sign of respect, and allowed me into their homes and into their lives.

I had never thought about the importance of place in one's life before I came here. The country I came from is a land of wanderers, my family more so than many others. Here, I saw the richness of belonging to family and community, their unquestioning support of each other during hard times, and the desire to pass on to one's children the joys of life's blessing in this place called home. Not that everyone finds this to be ideal—some do leave. But they leave *something*, and they can come back.

Daniella explained it to me. "When we have a funeral or a graduation or any big party, even the relatives in San José come."

I knew Ofelia when she was alive. She was old, frail and sometimes confused. Her husband had died, and her older children had left. Her youngest, Pablo, stayed and looked after her. She survived on a tiny government pension and support from Pablo, who worked at whatever odd jobs he could find. I sometimes hired him to pick fruit or cut weeds.

I was astonished when Pablo told me he had Chinese cousins in Chicago, the place I had called home before coming here.

Daniella confirmed his claim. "Ofelia and her husband adopted Pablo. His father was Chinese. His mother was an indigenous woman from the Zapaton Reserve."

Pablo was unquestionably a member of his community. I, however, felt like I had more in common with his wandering, biological family than I did with my current neighbors. I felt a vague loneliness and began to ask myself: *Where do I belong? Does this rolling stone need to stop and gather moss? Where is my moss?* I began spending more time in the urban areas near the capital where North American expats tend to cluster.

I slowly realized I need to be with people who know the places and the culture I have come from, and with whom I can share what is in my heart without having to pause to remember how to conjugate a verb. I treasure my friendships with *Ticos*, especially the *campesinos*. I am keeping the farm, but I have moved to a suburb of the capital and hope this is a place where I can sink roots and spread my branches.

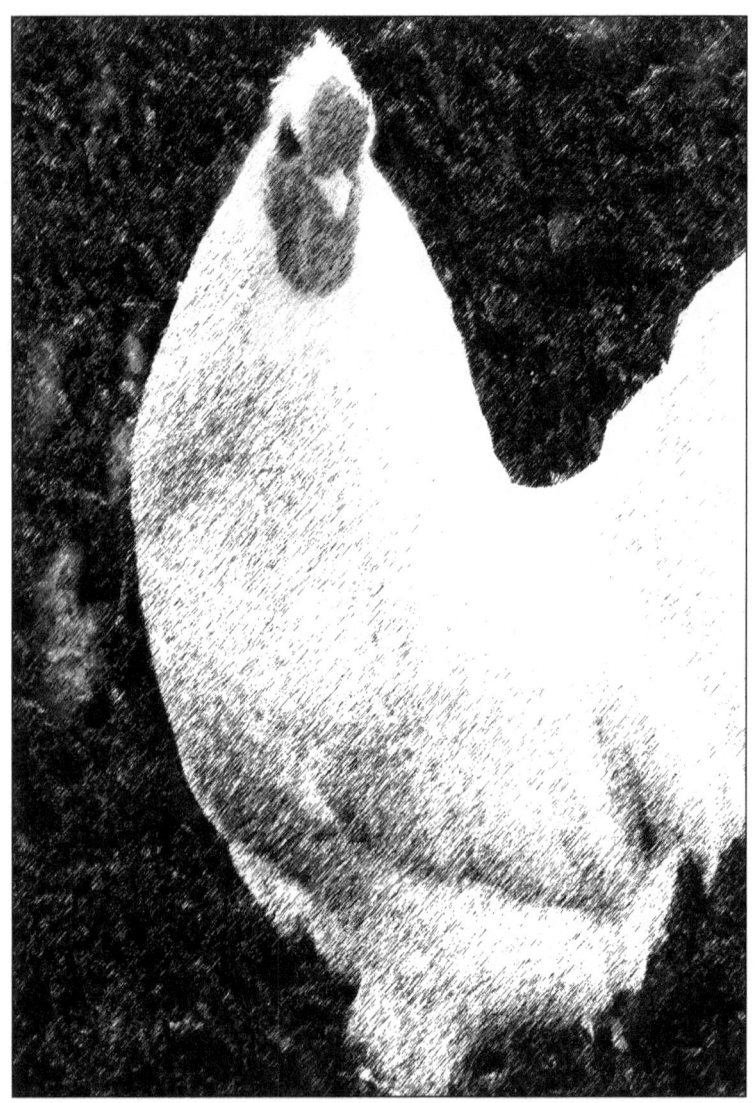

Chickens and Zippers

Lenny Karpman

In his 92nd year, Dad was suffering from advancing dementia. His rambling tales often included images of baby chicks, egg gathering and his mother's chicken soup. My wife Joan and I moved him out of his assisted-living quarters in Mill Valley, California, and brought him to our small farm in Costa Rica. His initial apprehension abated post-haste when we promised to provide him with chickens.

He was born in Russia in 1911. When he was a toddler, he fed the chickens on the family farm. Tevya, his father, immigrated to the United States in 1914 and sent money back every week. When, in 1916, Grandma Khana had enough saved, she sold the farm and trekked with six kids in tow across Siberia and Manchuria to Vladivostok, then to Yokohama, crossed the Pacific on a Japanese freighter, crossed the U.S. by train and eventually settled in a tenement in Hartford, Connecticut. There Dad raised Rhode Island reds on the roof and hatched fertile eggs on bags of salt, warmed in the oven by the pilot light. Charlie loved his little flock. His name in Russia had been Gdalya, but the milkman convinced his mother that he couldn't start school with such a foreign name. He was named Charlie after the milkman's horse.

He and his four brothers sold newspapers year round, caddied on weekends and holidays, and picked shade-grown tobacco during summer months under cheesecloth netting in stifling heat. Tobacco juice permeated their scalps and red clay caked in their nostrils, ears, and under their fingernails. Dad hated it and opted for more time at the local golf course, assisting the pro. He became a good golfer as a teenager and a golf instructor as a young adult. His father, Grandpa Tevya, worked fourteen hours a day in an Italian bakery, hauling sacks of flour as heavy as he was. Their combined efforts produced enough money for them to buy a modest house with a yard in which Dad built a coop and raised a dozen chickens, mostly for their eggs. Even though the eggs were smaller, brilliantly colored golden bantam hens and roosters were his love.

After high school, he moved to New York, worked as a runner for an insurance agency and went to City College of New York at night. He dreamed of owning a poultry farm as an avocation while pursuing an insurance career. The deepening Depression ended his schooling. He slept on a cot in his sister's livingroom back in Hartford and paid his share by working as a pelt cutter for a furrier, as a traveling salesman for a clothier, and as an instructor in a golf school.

When he met my mother, she was going to nursing school and sleeping on a sofa in her older sister's livingroom. They married and moved into a tiny apartment of their own. He went to work selling life insurance for Prudential. My sister and I were born in '36 and '38. Dad took us for rides in the country when we were toddlers. We gathered nuts, picked blueberries and sweet corn and visited his customers who raised geese, ducks, turkeys and chickens.

In 1944, Charlie appeared to have been bypassed by the draft. He was thirty-three and had two children. He bought a farm in Bloomfield, Connecticut, with chicken coops endowed with hot and cold running water and electricity. He beamed. He promised us red, gold and mahogany-colored goldenband fuzzy white Polish hens with tufted feet. Before we moved in, he was drafted into the navy. Mom cried. She lived in a city of 100,000 near her sisters and friends. She was frightened about the prospects of rural isolation as a solo parent. She had never driven a car and was phobic about learning. He sold the farm without a word.

When the draft age for married men with children was lowered from 34 to 32, he was discharged before he was ever deployed. The new owner wouldn't sell the farm back to Dad even for more money.

Mom and Dad lived in West Hartford for decades before moving to Ormond Beach, Florida. My sister and I settled in Atlanta and San Francisco, respectively.

Wandering in Costa Rica: Landscapes Lost and Found

Finally, when they were in their seventies, my parents moved to Northern California. Nearly every summer, we went to the Petaluma fairgrounds together so Dad could admire dozens of varieties of prize poultry. He often mused about finding a rural setting that could accommodate at least a few. Mom wouldn't hear of it. After she died, he no longer had the capacity for independent living. He began to fade. The administrators in his assisted-living residence suggested a nursing home. Joan and I offered him life on a farm instead.

In Costa Rica, we fenced off an area outside his bedroom, built a coop and adopted a small flock of poultry. They included reds, blacks, a pair of white Chinese silkies, a pair of guinea fowl and a lone rooster. He approved.

For the first six months, he wandered among them, gathered eggs and reminisced. Over the course of the subsequent twelve months, he watched the chickens less and less and spent more time sleeping and staring off into space. When he no longer recognized the chickens or any of us, we moved him into a pristine, sweet-smelling care facility in nearby La Garita called *Villa Alegria*, Happy House. The attentive Costa Rican staff treated him with compassion and respect. I visited him every other day. He was as pleasant to me as he was to anyone else, but he hadn't a notion that I was his son. I didn't badger him to try to remember.

At *Villa Alegria* he went thru a phase of disorientation that brought him back to adolescence. He repeatedly unzipped his fly and examined his penis and waved it at the other patients and staff. Had this behavior occurred back in California, he would have been summarily scolded, restrained and medicated into virtual coma. At *Villa Alegria* they put his pants on backwards so he couldn't get to his zipper. When he seemed frustrated or agitated, they gave him juice and cookies. He smiled every time. Charlie remained happy. About a month after his pants were reversed, he became mute. The only sound that seemed to coax a response from him was the crowing of a nearby rooster. When he heard it, he pursed his lips as if he were going to respond in kind.

Now I gather the eggs.

Lenny, After the Storm

Joanna Biggar

The last coffee cup washed,
the last wine glass emptied,
the last crumb swept,
Lenny drives the airport road
for the last time.
Dogs swarm the gate, barking,
lick their greetings.
He listens.
But the storm of voices,
seed clouds to make ideas rain,
has passed,
the writers' words consigned now
to bloom
into their quiet pages.

Somewhere in an unseen room
Lenny's wife, Joan,

Wandering in Costa Rica: Landscapes Lost and Found

sprinkles gentle silence
into the wind.
Lenny catches it
and enters the garden
at last alone.

Even the parrots and legless toucan
say nothing, cocking their
feathered heads
into question
marks.

He brushes the *camarones*—
yellow shrimp flowers with
white heads,
steps on St. Augustine grass,
springing back now beneath
the touch of his
solitary foot.
He nods to the *mano de tigre*,
the flowering almond,
the wild birds of paradise,
and walks beside the traveler's tree.
It bows to him.
Beneath the jacaranca,
he inhales,
and the wind catches

a first hint of nightfall,
star-petaled jasmine.

Above, hawks draw circles in the sky,
float over flame trees
burning the green flanks
of the western mountains.
Below, the Rio Segundo sings
its only song.

At a small white table
in the sheltering shade,
Lenny sits to listen.
There, in the chair opposite,
a shadow also sits
in silence.
The nameless boy
has come
to speak
without words,
to find Lenny
in his garden,
to find
the way home.

Glossary

abuela	grandmother
aves	birds
azul	blue
baño	bathroom
bodega	small grocery store
bahía	bay
campesino	farm worker
campo	countryside
Don	honorific title for men
Doña	honorific title for women
finca	farm, ranch
Finca Fango de la Suerte	Lucky Mud Farm
gallo	rooster
muchas gracias	thank you

Glossary

papel higiénico	toilet paper
peon	peasant
pez vela	swordfish
playa	beach
pupusa	Salvadoran dish of thick, handmade tortilla filled with cheese, beans, meat, etc.
rio	river
sueño azul	blue dream
terciopelo	fer de lance, a deadly snake
Tico	Costa Rican
Todos Santos	All Saints
tope	bump
Vientos de Navidad	Winds of Christmas

Author Biographies

Nancy Alpert was born in Long Beach, CA and transplanted to the Bay Area to attend rival schools Stanford and Berkeley. She graduated with an MSW, worked twenty years as a geropsychiatric social worker, and launched the Senior Peer Counseling program in San Francisco. When her career and marriage ended almost simultaneously, Nancy turned to writing. This lifelong hobby—evidenced by umpteen journals and a high school poetry award—led to her first publishing credit, an essay in *Venturing in Italy: Travels in Puglia, Land between Two Seas* (Traveler's Tales.) Along with essays and poetry, the children's picture book world calls her, enthralls her, and (so far) has stalled her. Nancy spends time at home with her nine-year-old daughter/editor; cats, Donut and Cupcake, and their edible namesakes; and an undisciplined Muse. She is still on the hunt for the best writing pen.

Greg Bascom, as a teenager, left Connecticut to work in Japan, Southeast Asia and South and Central America, first with the military and then with a multinational food company. Then he settled in an upscale suburb of San José with his Latina wife to write. His thriller *Lawless Elements*—emblazoned with robust characters, intriguing plot, and panoramas of an exotic land—won the 2009

Author Biographies

Faulkner-Wisdom novel competition. Read the first chapter of *Lawless* at www.GregBascom.com. With over thirty years living in Central America, Greg's stories and essays offer the reader multicolored perspectives on the reflections of culture.

Travel writer **Linda Lee Coffin** was raised as an Army brat and saw a lot of the world while growing up. She thus developed wanderlust and has continued to travel, publishing articles on wine and backroads touring. A retired U.S. federal employee, she has been a pilot, scuba diver and sailor. She lives on a ranch in California's wine country filled with rescued animals. She is also a part-time radio announcer and DJ on a PBS station in Northern California, featuring chill and New Age music. (nitetraveler2003@yahoo.com)

Lenny Karpman writes from his *finca* and refuge for birds and animals in Costa Rica's Central Valley. He has authored four books, several dozen articles, editorials, opinion pieces and reviews in magazines, newspapers and anthologies. His usual subjects are food, travel, civil liberties and human rights. He apprenticed at a French restaurant in San Francisco, practiced cardiology for more than thirty years and served on the boards and legislative policy committees for three large non-profits. He was editor of *San Francisco Medicine* and director of Northern California Kaiser Permanente's regional Cardiac Catheterization Laboratory. Lenny shares his life, happiness and wanderlust

Wandering in Costa Rica: Landscapes Lost and Found

with his wife, Joan Hall, JD. They have three adult children and six grandchildren.

Robin Kazmier is still paying off her expensive anthropology and geography degrees using a skill she learned in Georgia Public Schools and the barrios of Bolivia: Spanish. Robin has worked as a Study Abroad Adviser, Medical Spanish Instructor, and Volunteer Coordinator on a cocoa farm in Costa Rica. When not working, she can be found scuba diving, backpacking, snowshoeing, making religious pilgrimages, experimenting with medicinal plants, and always, writing. She has a long history of journaling furiously about her adventures in Latin America, but professionally her writings mostly include academic material meant to prepare students for cultural immersion and conducting research abroad. She now primarily writes for *Common Ground International*'s blog on Latino Culture and Spanish Language in the workplace

Robin has recently returned to Costa Rica after her previous two-year stint on a cocoa farm there. She is involved in a variety of projects, from co-managing a bed & breakfast (www.rainforestdreamscostarica.com) to working with groups of medical professionals who come to Costa Rica to learn medical Spanish and provide healthcare in underserved communities. However, her next endeavor—the one that brought her back—will be to re-start her own natural soap/cleaning products business, inspired by her friends in

Author Biographies

the countryside who are without municipal water treatment. http://commongroundinternational.blogspot.com/).

Nature nut abhors long walks on the beach, fears fatal bug bites, enjoys taxidermy. **Laurie McAndish King** has always loved the wild, but is not always a good judge of safe distances. She has tracked lions on foot—without a gun—in Botswana; chased lemurs through the mountains of Madagascar; fended off leeches in tropical Queensland; and banded sharp-taloned raptors in Northern California.

Laurie has an undergraduate degree in philosophy, earned a master's degree in online education, and is developing a natural history-based iPhone application. She pays the bills with her marketing consulting practice. Laurie's essays have aired on radio and been published in magazines and literary anthologies, most recently Travelers' Tales' *Best Women's Travel Writing 2009*. Her photography won first place in *Smithsonian* magazine's 2010 international photo contest.

Laurie also wrote *An Erotic Alphabet* and co-edited two volumes of erotica in the *Hot Flashes: sexy little stories and poems series*. Reach her at www.LaurieMcAndishKing.com.

Thanasis Maskaleris was born in Arkadia, Greece and immigrated to the U.S. at the age of 17. He studied Philosophy and English at the University of Oklahoma, and Comparative Literature at Indiana University and the UC-Berkeley. He has written original poetry in Greek and in English, and has translated contemporary Greek poetry and prose extensively.

Thanasis taught Comparative Literature and Creative Writing at San Francisco State University, until his recent retirement. At SFSU he was also the Founding Director of the Center for Modern Greek Studies and spearheaded the establishment of the Nikos Kazantzakis Chair. His most recent publication (co-edited/translated with Nanos Valaoritis) is *An Anthology of Modern Greek Poetry*.

He is translator/editor of the forthcoming *The Terrestrial Kazantzaki—The Saviors of the Earth*, an anthology of passages about nature and the workers of the soil—intended to inspire ecological action.

Carol McCool's first published work was her doctoral dissertation for her Ed.D. in educational psychology. For many years, her writing served her career as a psychologist and educator.

Several years ago, Carol moved to a small farm in the mountains of Costa Rica in an area that still reflects the culture and lifestyle of decades long past. With an open heart and inquisitive mind, she writes about her travel and expat experiences and the fascinating people in her tiny village. A freelance contributor to local English-language periodicals, including *The Tico Times,* she has published seventeen feature stories, personal essays, and shorter pieces. She has ten new stories about to be published in the anthology, *Costa*

Author Biographies

Rican Kaleidoscope, by the group of writers known as The Bards of Paradise.

A peace activist and environmentalist, Carol's passions include writing about organic, sustainable methods of food production. She longs for a world in which every country provides food security for its own people, and humankind lives in harmony with the earth.

She is the owner of Rainforest Dreams, a newly opened bed-and-breakfast near the nation's capital (www.rainforestdreamscostarica.com).

Life lover adores long walks on beaches, abhors mosquito bites, and attempts the salsa. **Mary Jean Pramik**, a coalminer's daughter and a great-great granddaughter of the Mongolian plane, has often coveted the free spirit of dancing in the wild, yet has spent most of her life keeping a safe distance from such experiences. She has hitchhiked across the United States, chased children through wet mountains in Marin, fended off bill collectors in San Francisco, and counted sharp-taloned dead birds along Point Reyes sands in Northern California. Communicating with hoards of screeching penguins in Antarctica remains a high point in her sojourn on this planet.

MJ Pramik earned both undergraduate and graduate degrees in biological sciences, and currently is completing her MFA in Writing. She moonlights as a medical writer, penning such scientific thrillers as *Norenthindrone: The First Three*

Decades, the fast-paced history of the first birth control pill extracted from a Mexican yam. Winner of the coveted Mary Womer Medal, MJ Pramik's articles and essays have appeared in *Nature Biotechnology, Drug Topics,* and *Cosmetic Surgery News,* and mainstream publications such as *Good Housekeeping, Odyssey,* and the *National Enquirer.* She has contributed to the *Venturing* travel series on the Canal du Midi, Southern Greece, Southern Ireland, and Puglia, Italy.

Anne Sigmon flunked jump rope in 7th grade and washed out of college PE. After college, she headed for San Francisco and a career in corporate public relations. Exotic travel was the stuff of dreams until, at 38, she married Jack, took tea with erstwhile headhunters in Borneo and climbed Mt. Kilimanjaro at 43. Five years later, she was zapped by a career-ending stroke caused by an obscure autoimmune disease called Antiphospholipid Syndrome (APS). She may be stuck with blood thinners and a fuddly brain, but she's still traveling to isolated regions ranging from Botswana to Burma and, most recently, to a remote rainforest in Costa Rica. Anne's personal essays have appeared in local and national publications including *Good Housekeeping* and *Stroke Connection* magazines. She is currently working on a book about her experience with stroke and autoimmune disease.

Editor Biographies

Joanna Biggar is a teacher, writer and traveler whose special places of the heart include the California coast and the South of France. She has degrees in Chinese and French and, as a professional writer for twenty-five years, has written poetry, fiction, personal essays, features, news and travel articles for hundreds of publications including *The Washington Post Magazine, Psychology Today, The International Herald Tribune,* and *The Wall Street Journal.* Her book *Travels and Other Poems* was published in 1996, and her most recent travel essays have appeared in the *Venturing* series, whose anthologies include books on France, Greece, Ireland and Italy. A novel, *That Paris Year*, is to be published by ASP books in 2010. She has taught journalism, creative writing, personal essay and travel writing since 1984 in many venues, most recently in Costa Rica, where she also enrolled in Spanish language school. She has also taught reading and writing at St. Martin de Porres Middle School and Emiliano Zapata Street Academy in Oakland, California, where she lives. (jobiggar@gmail.com)

Editor Biographies

Poet, travel writer, and novelist **Linda Watanabe McFerrin** has been traveling since she was two and writing about it since she was six. She is a contributor to numerous magazines and anthologies. She is the author of two poetry collections, past editor of a popular Northern California guidebook and a winner of the Katherine Anne Porter Prize for Fiction. Her novel, *Namako: Sea Cucumber*, was named Best Book for the Teen-Age by the New York Public Library. In addition to authoring an award-winning short story collection, *The Hand of Buddha*, she has co-edited several anthologies, including the *Hot Flashes: sexy little stories & poems* series.

Linda has judged the San Francisco Literary Awards and the Kiriyama Prize, served as a visiting mentor for the Loft Mentor Series and been guest faculty at the Oklahoma Arts Institute. A past NEA Panelist and juror for the Marin Literary Arts Council, she has mentored a long list of accomplished authors toward publication.

Her newest book, *Dead Love*, a novel about Japan and zombies is due out from Stone Bridge Press in September of 2010. (www.lwmcferrin.com)

www.ingramcontent.com/pod-product-compliance
Lightning Source LLC
Chambersburg PA
CBHW070616300426
44113CB00010B/1557